THE REFRACTIVE THINKER®

An Anthology of Higher Learning

THE REFRACTIVE THINKER®

An Anthology of Higher Learning

VOL II
Research Methodology

Third Edition: Effective Research Methods & Designs for Doctoral Scholars

Foreword by Jim Kouzes and Barry Posner

The Refractive Thinker® Press
9065 Big Plantation Avenue
Las Vegas, NV 89143-5440 USA

Info@refractivethinker.com
Http://www.refractivethinker.com

Books are available through The Refractive Thinker® Press at special discounts for bulk purchases for the purpose of sales promotion, seminar attendance, or educational purposes. Special volumes can be created for specific purposes and to organizational specifications. Please contact us for further details.

Orders placed on http://www.refractivethinker.com for students and military receive a 15% discount.

Copyright©2013 by The Refractive Thinker® Press
Managing Editor: Dr. Cheryl A. Lentz

Library of Congress Control Number: 2013945437

Volume ISBNs
    Soft Cover   978-0-9883324-2-3
    E-book/PDF   978-0-9883324-3-0
    *Kindle and electronic versions available

Refractive Thinker® logo by Joey Root, The Refractive Thinker® Press logo design by Jacqueline Teng, cover design Sheila Stewart International.

Printed in the United States of America

Volume II (3rd ed.)
10 9 8 7 6 5 4 3 2 1

CONTENTS

DEDICATION

If the mind is to emerge unscathed from the relentless struggle with the unforeseen, two qualities are dispensable: first, an intellect that even in the darkest hour, retains some glimmer of the inner light which leads to the truth; and second, the courage to follow this light, wherever it may lead.

~Carl von Clausewitz

FOREWORD

As the refractive thinker . . .

The key messages that a reader looks to this series is two fold. First, the books in this series are not meant to be a just another textbook. The goal of this series is not definition but application and unique application of various methods and designs. These scholars are those on the cutting edge of research, finding new ways of application in the how to conduct research. Each of these authors has a unique twist to their research, what they did and why they did it in a particular way. We know that academia is rather traditional and change comes slowly. These doctors took a bit of a risk to not only forge ahead with new research but new ways of conducting research that challenges the status quo.

Second the goal is to have the reader learn from those that have gone before them, to shorten the reader's learning curve as contributions are made to the greater body of knowledge within research. These authors share their thoughts on what they did and why, and what they recommend doing different for the reader in following their path. These authors do not only ask why, they ask why not? Think Einstein. If thinking is inside the box, and critical thinking is outside the box, refractive thinking is asking the question of what lies beyond the box.

Jim Kouzes and Barry Posner
Leavey School of Business, Santa Clara University
Authors of The Leadership Challenge
www.leadershipchallenge.com

PREFACE

I think therefore I am.
–Renee Descartes

I CRITICALLY THINK TO BE.
I THINK REFRACTIVELY TO CHANGE THE WORLD.

WELCOME TO THE REFRACTIVE THINKER®
VOLUME II: RESEARCH METHODOLOGY THIRD EDITION

Thank you for joining us for the Summer 2013 edition, as we continue to celebrate the accomplishments of doctoral educators affiliated with many phenomenal institutions of higher learning. The purpose of this offering within the anthology series is to share another glimpse into the scholarly works of these participating authors, specifically about the topic of research methodology. The goal is to add to the first two editions of Volume II with additional unique and innovative applications of research methods. The purpose is to provide a resource beyond the conventional boundaries of an academic textbook, providing individual chapters that students and faculty may consider when choosing various research methods and designs as part of the doctoral dissertation.

This peer-reviewed resource offers a framework that presents key categories of research to include the three main Methods: Quantitative, Qualitative, and Mixed Methods to include many designs that include correlational, case study, comparative study, the Delphi technique, phenomenology, the van Kaam method, and a new method debuts—the PDAI, all of which are unique in their overall structure and application. Further, these approaches reflect the construct of the refractive thinker in which each author challenged the conventional wisdom and expanded beyond the traditional boundaries. These authors dared not to just think outside the box. Instead, the box continues to evolve into exploring nearly entirely new ideas for construction of 'the box,' such as applicable methods or perhaps elimination of the traditional box completely.

The Refractive Thinker is an intimate expression of who we are—the ability to think beyond the traditional boundaries of thinking and critical thinking. Instead of mere reflection and evaluation, one challenges the very boundaries of the constructs itself. If thinking is *inside* the box, and critical thinking is *outside* the box, we add the next step of refractive thinking, *beyond* the box. Perhaps the need exists to dissolve the box completely. As in our first nine volumes, the authors within these pages are on a mission to change the world through research. Scholars are never satisfied or quite content with *what is* or asking *why*; instead these authors intentionally strive to push and test the limits to ask *why not*.

Embrace this next adventure of *The Refractive Thinker* in which this third edition of Volume II continues the discussion begun several years ago. These prior works included *The Delphi Primer* as well as sections that included mixed methods, qualitative, and quantitative methods, as well as a few new designs. Remember not only do we offer three volumes for your consideration for your doctoral studies and choices regarding methods and design, but also 32 individual e-Chapters are also available thought our website http://www.refractivethinker.com as well as through your Kindle via Amazon should you desire to only select your favorites.

Please contact The Refractive Thinker® Press for further information regarding these authors and the works contained within these pages. Perhaps you or your organization may be looking for their expertise to incorporate as part of your annual corporate meetings as a keynote or guest speaker(s), or to offer individual or group seminars, coaching, or consultation.

We look forward to your interest in discussing future opportunities. This collection of authors will continue journey that began with volume I. Come join us in the quest to be refractive thinkers and add your wisdom to the collection. We look forward to your stories.

ACKNOWLEDGEMENTS

The foundation of scholarly research embraces the art of asking questions—to validate and affirm *what* we do and *why*. Though asking the right questions, the right answers are found. Leaders often challenge this status quo, to offer alternatives and new directions, to dare to try something that has not yet been done as again proved true in this case with our third edition of Volume II. This publication required the continued belief in this new publishing model by those willing to continue forward on this voyage. As a result, please let me express my gratitude for the help of the many that made this collaboration possible.

First, let me offer a special thank you to Trish Hladek for her unwavering support and belief that traversing unchartered waters is worthy of the journey. My gratitude extends to our Peer Review Board to include: Dr. Patricia D'Urso, Dr. Judy Fisher Blando, and Dr Tom Woodruff; and our Board of Directors to include: Dr. Judy Fisher-Blando, Dr. Tom Woodruff, and myself. In addition, let me offer a well deserved thank you to our production specialist, Sheila Stewart and her team; Refractive Thinker® logo designer, Joey Root; and our cover designer team, at Sheila Stewart International and companion website designer consulting team, Tom Antion and Associates.

Let me also extend my sincere gratitude to all participating authors within The Refractive Thinker* series who continue to believe in this project as we continue to expand our program. We appreciate their commitment to leadership and to the concept of what it means to be a refractive thinker.

Dr. Cheryl A. Lentz
Managing Editor
Las Vegas, NV
September 2013

CHAPTER 1

University Endowments in Financial Crisis:
Making the Grade or Academic Probation?

By Dr. Ellen Beattie

Endowment funds compose a significant component of an institution's financial health. Endowments serve three purposes in higher education institutions; (a) to give institutions greater independence, (b) to provide operational stability, and (c) to produce educational excellence (Swenson, 2009). During the Financial Crisis of 2008 and 2009, American institutions lost 18.7% of their endowment values from

June 30, 2008 to June 30, 2009 (National Association of College and University Business Officers-Commonfund Study of Endowments [NCSE], 2011a). Significant monetary losses reduce an institution's ability to (a) provide high levels of instructional effectiveness, (b) support students financially, and (c) invest in technological and campus innovations (Altbach et al., 2009; Doyle & Delaney, 2009; Swenson, 2009). Significant endowment losses coincided with global economic slowing, credit market tightening, and reduction in government support, challenging the ability to fund higher education endeavors adequately (Altbach et al., 2009). With their core missions in jeopardy, higher education administrators must evaluate the relationship between institutional and endowment characteristics and endowment investment performance. Innovative, refractive thinking employed to understand the effects of significant capital market downturns on endowments is necessary. This chapter includes the research methodology applied to the 2012 Beattie study, *A Quantitative Correlation Study: Institutional Characteristics and Endowment Investment Performance Following the 2008 – 2009 Financial Crisis.*

Overview

Institutions of higher education must remain financially solvent to meet their mission of creating productive learning environments for their students. The primary component of an institution's wealth is the value of the endowment fund. The purpose of this quantitative correlation study was to measure the relationship between institutional characteristics and endowment investment performance in institutions of higher education in the United States, following the dramatic endowment monetary losses during and since the fiscal year ending in 2009. The sample included 724 higher education institutions within the United States. The analyses of data provided descriptive and inferential statistics. Spearman's rank-order correlation and multiple regression analysis were used to measure the correlations between endowment investment performance and institutional characteristics and endowment investment performance and institutional characteristics. The results of the current research revealed that no statistically significant relationship existed between endowment investment performance and institutional characteristics (Adjusted $R^2(18)$= .00, p = .50) or endowment investment performance and endowment characteristics (Adjusted $R^2(18)$ = .00, p = .50). The Beattie (2012) study added to the body of knowledge of higher education financial stability and endowment investment growth. Implications of the study include the identification of the diversity in institutional wealth and endowment performance and the dramatic effects of capital market fluctuations on endowment market values.

Background and Theory

Based on the theory of intergenerational equality, endowment funds support a balance between current and future institutional needs. Vigilant management of endowments ensures the funds can support the current spending needs and preserve the fund's purchasing power for future generations. In the short-term, endowments contribute to the operating budget and the capital budget of an institution (Yeager, Nelson, Potter, Weidman, & Zullo, 2001).

Well-managed endowment funds contribute to current and future financial stability by generating a consistent and reliable source of income. When revenue sources such as government support or alumni contributions decrease, endowment income can support educational endeavors. The income supports specific academic programs, provides institutional aid to students, and improves campus facilities. Generating this income increasingly requires expert investment knowledge, financial sophistication, and persistent oversight.

In the first decade of the 21st century, increases in higher education costs, decreases in public allocations, and the public's awareness of and sensitivity to tuition increases jeopardized financial stability for educational institutions (Eckel & Kezar, 2003). Concurrently, changes in the global economic climate negatively influenced endowment fund growth and investment performance. Significant endowment losses mirrored global economic slowing, credit market tightening, and government support reductions, challenging the ability to fund higher education endeavors adequately (Altbach et al., 2009).

Refractive thinking permits analysis without traditional boundaries. Without limits, research examines problems from pioneering mindsets. The specific problem addressed in the Beattie (2012) study was that endowment losses experienced in the fiscal year 2009 affected the economic stability of U.S. higher education in fiscal year 2010. In an already strained financial environment, diminished endowment returns presented challenges for functional areas of higher education. Losses to endowment funds, less alumni and corporate giving, and cuts in federal and state support have had a direct influence on the operating budgets of institutions (Yeager et al., 2001). Increased investments in illiquid assets and a more conservative credit and lending environment challenge the financial stability of institutions, delaying capital investments in technology and campus infrastructure (Chabotar, 2010; Karmin & Hechinger, 2008).

Less stability in an institution's finances directly affects students and the institution's quest for excellence (Swenson, 2009). Institutional leaders examined cost cutting measures to lessen their operating budget deficits, but increased class size, use of part-time faculty, hiring freezes, and staff and service reductions threaten academic effectiveness, campus morale, and quality of student life (Altbach et al., 2009; Doyle & Delaney, 2009). Tuition discounting, funded and diminished by endowment returns, has lessened the ability to attract and retain quality students. The purpose of the current quantitative study was to examine the relationship between institutional and endowment characteristics and endowment investment performance in 724 U.S. institutions of higher education.

Data Analysis Methodology

The goal of the study was to measure the extent to which institutional characteristics and endowment characteristics may be related to endowment investment performance, specifically in the year following a significant capital market decline. The quantitative approach permitted hypothesis testing and determined the probability of acceptance or rejection of the null hypothesis with inferential statistics. Beattie (2012) chose a quantitative research approach as the most appropriate for the current study based on operational definitions, narrow and focused research questions, and statistical analysis to test for relationships (Vogt, 2007). According to Neuman (2006), quantitative research adheres to a linear path with a sequence of fixed steps. The research topic and questions guided the study design planning, measurement of variables, sampling, data collection, and analysis.

Appropriate for the Beattie (2012) study, the quantitative research approach included the measurement of variables publicly available in numeric form. The published numeric data permitted the testing of the study's hypotheses. The choice of relevant variables, a precise manner of measurement, a quality sample and effective design of the study strengthened the confidence of the quantitative research results (Cooper & Schindler, 2011; Firestone, 1987). The quantitative research approach permitted a logical plan for data collection and analysis.

Data Collection

The reliability of a study depends on the validity of the data collected. All data collected for this study were secondary data available from public sources. For each institution of higher education in the sample, the net change in investment returns from fiscal year 2009 to 2010 was calculated, and data on institutional characteristics for the corresponding year were collected. Data collection occurred from the following three primary sources: Guidestar Database, Integrated Postsecondary Education Data System (IPEDS), and the Carnegie Foundation for the Advancement of Teaching.

The period associated with the data collected for the study was vital to the study goal. The examination of the extent of the relationship between institutional characteristics, endowment characteristics, and endowment investment performance in the year of the significant market decline of fiscal year ending in 2009 and the following year required precise data collection. The period of interest included the fiscal years 2009 and 2010, spanning July 1, 2008 until June 30, 2010. The 2009 Internal Revenue Service Form 990, providing the financial data and data on the governing board, aligned with this time period. When collecting information on institutional characteristics, the academic year 2009-2010 most closely aligned with the period of interest.

Dependent Variable-Endowment Investment Performance

Data for the dependent variable were from the 2009 Internal Revenue Service Form 990. The Internal Revenue Service require the annual submission of the *Return of Organization Exempt from Income Tax* form to the Department of the Treasury-Internal Revenue Service. The form provides in-depth financial data about nonprofit organizations and is publicly available through an online nonprofit database, Guidestar. Section V on Schedule D *Supplemental Financial Statements* included the necessary information (Guidestar, 2011).

The net change in endowment investment performance was calculated from the raw endowment data. To normalize the endowment investment performance data, the raw data required manipulation. To account for the differences in endowment funds size, the fiscal year 2009 beginning endowment value was given a value of 1.00. The 2009 investment percent gain or loss was applied to obtain the ending 2009 value.

The process was repeated with the 2010 beginning balance and the 2010 endowment investment performance percent gain or loss. The process produced a multiplier of 1.00 indicating the ending balance following the 2-year endowment investment performance from the original balance. A value of 1.00 indicated no change in endowment. A value less than 1.00 indicated an investment loss from the beginning balance and a value greater than 1.00 indicated an investment gain.

Independent Variables

The independent variables included 12 institutional and endowment characteristics. Independent variables included institutional characteristics (control, institutional type, governing bodies, religious affiliation, geographic location, tuition levels, student enrollment, selectivity, tuition discounting through institutional aid) and endowment characteristics (endowment size, contributions, and the percentage of total endowment designated as permanent endowment). The use of these variables required collection of a wide range of institutional data demonstrating the large variances in institutional and endowment characteristics in the sample. All information was available publicly through the U.S. Department of Education National Center for Education Statistics, *the* Carnegie Foundation for the Advancement of Teaching, and the nonprofit Guidestar database.

Data Analysis

The data analysis process facilitated the interpretation of the data with respect to the study research questions. In this quantitative correlation study, the data analysis involved measuring the extent of the relationship between the independent and dependent variables. Descriptive statistics describe simple patterns in the data and include measures of central tendency (mean, median, mode) and measures of spread (range, standard deviation) (Neuman, 2006). Inferential statistics allow data to be gathered on a relatively small sample and statistical tests used to infer results applicable to a larger population (Creswell, 2012). In correlation studies, statistical tests are conducted with numerical data to determine the strength and direction of the correlation between the variables studied (Creswell, 2012).

Frequencies and Descriptive Statistics

Frequency analysis helps identify general trends in the data. Frequencies for the nominal variables in the current study were computed. The nominal variables included control, institutional type, religious affiliation, and geographic location. Tables and charts were used to summarize findings about the composition of the sample and primary trends in the results. Correlation analysis in SPSS statistical software required the use of dummy coding. Dummy coding involves assigning nominal variables a numeric code (Cooper & Schindler, 2011). Nominal variables coded as 0 and 1 create dummy variables for an effective system.

Descriptive statistics simply describe the data within the sample with calculations of the mean, median, mode, minimum, maximum, and standard deviations (Neuman, 2006). The descriptive statistics presented a comprehensive understanding of the sample's characteristics. These statistics were calculated for the independent variables of governing bodies, tuition level, student enrollment, selectivity, and tuition discounting, all of the endowment characteristics, and the dependent variable of endowment investment performance.

Correlation Analysis

Exploratory data analysis and data visualization provided an initial exploration and examination of the study variables. The Statistical Package for Social Sciences (SPSS version 20) was used to calculate the statistical data pertaining to correlation. Before conducting statistical tests, data must be checked to ensure that no assumptions of the statistical tests are violated. In the descriptive data analysis, four variables were identified with a high skew. According to Rea and Parker (2005), each variable's skew should not exceed ± 2 to be considered normally distributed. Governing body, endowment size, contributions, and the dependent variable, net change in endowment investment performance, were identified with skew values over ± 2 and could not be considered normally distributed.

Parametric tests require an assumption of normal distribution. In this study, a nonparametric test was needed in the bivariate analysis conducted between the dependent variable and the independent variables because of the skewness of the dependent variable. The highly skewed dependent variable required that Spearman's *rho*, which is sensitive to skew, rather than Pearson's *r*, be used to test for significant correlations (Larson & Farber, 2006). The Spearman's ranked correlation coefficient was chosen because it does not assume normality and was conducted between the study dependent and independent variables. Spearman's rank-order correlation is appropriate for skewed data because the calculation does not use the mean of the data in the calculation and is robust to outliers (Cooper & Schindler, 2011).

Spearman's ranked correlation coefficient range from - 1 to 0 to + 1. The strength of a correlation is determined by how close the coefficient is to either a positive or negative 1. Positive relationships indicate that as one variable increases, so does the other variable. In an inverse relationship, one variable increases as the other decreases. The closer the correlation coefficient is to one, the stronger the relationship between the two variables. Correlations within the range of -.50 to .50 signify weak relationships (Creswell, 2012).

Determinations made before the correlation analysis included the choice of one- or two-tailed tests, dummy coding, and the level of significance for rejecting the null hypothesis. The study nondirectional hypotheses required two-tailed tests. Dummy coding was necessary for the nominal variables to be used in the correlation analysis. The process of coding information is assigning a numerical value to nominal data (Creswell, 2008).

Control, type, geographic location, and religion were dummy coded. Numeric coding of 0 and 1 were used in place of the categorical names. The null hypotheses are rejected if statistically significant results are found (Creswell, 2008). Failure to reject the null occurs if the statistical tests produce no significant findings. In the current study, a probability level of $p \leq .05$ was used as the criteria for rejecting or failing to reject the null hypothesis.

The appropriate choice of multiple regression analysis assessed the relationship between the dependent variable and multiple independent variables (Vogt, 2007). Multiple regression analysis identified how the institutional and endowment characteristics related to endowment investment performance. Multiple regression analysis generates a measure of the combined relationship and usefulness of the independent variables on the dependent variable (Vogt, 2007).

Multiple regression analysis to measure the combined effect of the associated independent variables from each research question provided responses to RQ1 and RQ2. The adjusted coefficient of determination R^2 measured the proportion of the variation in the dependent variable accounted for by the independent variables and provided information on the effect size (Creswell, 2012).

Based on the R^2 that reflects the "amount of common variance" (p. 498) between two variables, the adjusted R^2 was considered an accurate measure of goodness of fit because the statistic corrects for the number of independent variables (Cooper & Schindler, 2011).

Findings

The first step in data analysis was computing frequencies for the nominal variables. Four of the nine institutional characteristics were nominal variables, including control, type, religion, and geographic location. Within the sample, 69% (n = 489) of the institutions were privately controlled and 31% (n = 220) were publicly controlled. Master's degrees were the most frequently reported types of degree offered by institutions (n = 235, 33%). Non-religiously affiliated institutions constituted 64% (n = 451) of the institutions in the sample. The sample included institutions from nine geographic regions of the United States. The regions with the largest number of institutions included in the sample were the Mideast (n = 165, 23%) and the Southeast (n = 162, 22%). The Inter American University of Puerto Rico was the only institution (n = 1, 0%) in the outlying region.

A review of the descriptive statistics provides general information about the study data. Descriptive statistics were calculated for the interval-level variables. These included the independent variables of governing bodies, tuition level, student enrollment, selectivity, and tuition discounting, all of the endowment characteristics, and the dependent variable of endowment investment performance. Descriptive statistics for interval-level variables included number in the sample, mean, standard deviation, skew, minimum, and maximum.

Institutional Characteristics

Descriptive statistics were calculated for the five interval-level institutional characteristic variables. These variables included governing bodies, tuition level, student enrollment, selectivity, and tuition discounting. The institutions contained in the sample had an average governing board member of 32 (n = 724).

The institution with the lowest tuition rate, Berea College, (n = 633, $9,196) and with the highest tuition rate, Georgetown University (n = 633, $54,954) demonstrated the large disparity of educational costs to students across the sample. The difference between the smallest student enrollment (n = 690, 110) and the largest student enrollment (n = 690, 68,064) also demonstrated the diversity of the sample. The percentage admitted in 2009 averaged 63% (n = 619). In 69% (n = 660) of the institutions, institutional-level financial aid was provided to first-year students.

Endowment Characteristics

Examination of the descriptive statistics of the endowment characteristics of the sample institutions demonstrated large disparities in institutional wealth. Interval-level data described each endowment characteristic. The institutions ranged in endowment values from $620,199 to $16,863,612,000 with a mean of $310,636,518 ($n$ = 724). Yale University, the institution with the highest endowment value, has 54 times the average institution endowment value. Contributions to the endowment funds ranged from $-1,683,209 to 869,169,000 (n = 724).

Endowment Investment Performance

The net change in endowment investment performance spanned on a continual range from .57 (University of Wisconsin Foundation) to 1.97 (Vaughn College of Aeronautics and Technology). Beginning with a fictional $100,000, the 2-year cycle would have allowed the

University of Wisconsin Foundation to have an ending balance of $57,000 and the Vaughn College of Aeronautics and Technology to have an ending balance of $197,000. A difference of $140,000 would separate the endowment funds of the two institutions. Any net change in endowment investment performance below 1.00 indicated that the fiscal year 2010 ending balance was lower than the 2009 beginning balance. Of the 724 institutions included in the sample, 641 had ending 2010 balances lower than their beginning 2009 balance.

Correlations

The first research question measured the relationship between institutional characteristics and investment performance. Six variables were statistically significant with net change in endowment investment performance. The correlations were significant, but the effects were small. Control was statistically significant with net change in endowment investment performance. The correlation was negative and weak $(r_s(18)= -.09, p = .01)$. Under institutional type, associate and doctorate were statistically significant with net change in endowment investment performance.

The correlation between associate institutions and net change in endowment investment performance was positive and weak $(r_s(18)= .12, p = .001)$. The correlation between doctorate institutions and net change in endowment investment performance was negative and weak $(r_s(18)= -.08, p = .03)$. A statistically significant correlation between governing body and net change in endowment investment performance was negative and weak $(r_s(18)= -.09, p = .02)$.

Two negative and weak correlations existed between tuition levels and dependent variable $(r_s(18)= -.12, p = .001)$ and tuition discounting and the dependent variable $(r_s(18) = -.12, p = .001)$. No other statistically significant correlations existed. The effects of the correlations were small and too weak to reject the null hypothesis. The null hypothesis of no significant relationship existing between institutional characteristics and endowment investment performance was accepted.

Multiple regression analysis was used to test if the institutional characteristics significantly related to net change in endowment investment performance. Multiple regression indicated the combined effect of the nine institutional variables did not significantly relate to the net change in endowment investment performance (Adjusted $R^2(18)$= .00, p = .50). A second regression was run with only the institutional characteristics that had significant individual correlations.

The second multiple regression indicated the combined effect of the five institutional variables with statistically significant individual correlations (control, associate degrees, doctoral and research degrees, tuition level, and tuition discounting) did not significantly relate to the net change in endowment investment performance (Adjusted $R^2(18)$ = .00, p = .50). The adjusted R^2 finding provided empirical support for the null hypothesis indicating a lack of significant relationship between institutional characteristics and endowment investment performance.

The Beattie (2012) study's second research question measured the relationship between endowment characteristics and investment performance. A negative and weak statistically significant correlation was found between endowment size and net change in endowment investment performance ($r_s(3)$= - .18, p = .001). The correlation between contributions and net change in endowment was statistically significant but weak ($r_s(3)$= - .14, p = .001). The correlation between permanent endowment and net change in endowment investment performance was not statistically significant.

The effects of the correlations were small and too weak to reject the null hypothesis. The null hypothesis of no significant relationship existing between endowment characteristics and endowment investment performance was accepted. Multiple regression analysis indicated the combined effect of the three endowment variables (size, contributions, and percentage of permanent endowment) did not significantly relate to the net change in endowment investment performance (Adjusted R^2 (3) = .00, p = .52). The adjusted R^2 finding provided empirical support for the null hypothesis indicating a lack of significant relationship between endowment characteristics and endowment investment performance.

In summary, the analysis of frequencies and descriptive statistics led to the identification of general trends in the data. Computing the frequencies of the four nominal variables (control, type, religion, and geographic location) showed a widely diverse sample. Descriptive data pertaining to the study nine interval-level variables (governing bodies, tuition level, student enrollment, selectivity, and tuition discounting, the endowment characteristics of endowment size, contributions, and the percentage of total endowment designated as permanent endowment) and the dependent variable (endowment investment performance) supported the vast institutional diversity. The data indicated large disparities in institutional wealth in the sample institutions.

The first research question asked, *To what extent is there a relationship between institutional characteristics and endowment investment performance?* The second research question asked, *To what extent is there a relationship between endowment characteristics and endowment investment performance?* Spearman's rank order correlation and multiple regression analysis were performed. Based on the data collected and analyzed, no strong statistically significant and strong relationships exist between endowment investment performance and institutional characteristics or between endowment investment performance and endowment characteristics. All effects were small, and the null hypotheses could not be rejected. The two null hypotheses of the study were that no relationships exist between endowment investment performance and institutional characteristics or between endowment investment performance and endowment characteristics. Failure to reject both hypotheses of the study means that endowment investment performance is not statistically significantly related to institutional characteristics or endowment characteristics.

The findings of this study indicate large differences in an institution's ability to recover from the dramatic endowment losses of fiscal year 2009. The data suggested endowment net change ranging from .57 to 1.97 in the 2-year period studied. This disparity suggests either institutional differences or endowment management differences to account for the large variations in endowment fund investment performance. The effects of the relationships were too small to indicate any significant relationship between the dependent and the independent variables. The lack of significant relationship between these variables suggests that other factors might contribute to an endowment's fund investment performance. Possibly, no relationships were found because other factors such as external management of funds and investment in alternative assets classes relate to endowment growth more strongly. The body of literature reveals that institutional leaders are choosing external management because of increase in the complexity of asset allocation decisions and investment choices (Humphreys, 2010). Many institutions invest in alternative asset classes such as private equity, using more high-risk, high-reward investing vehicles (Swenson, 2009). These two factors create an environment in which endowment investment returns are mirroring the United States' capital markets. Expecting positive endowment performance in lagging capital markets or dramatically different returns than their counterparts might be unrealistic. Institutional leaders cannot support the mission of the institution without necessary funding, making endowment research and the institutional and endowment characteristics that affect endowment growth critically important to examine. Institutional leaders must focus on strategies that aid in understanding endowment growth and maximizing investment performance.

Conclusion

The refractive thought process encouraged an innovative study of endowment performance during significant capital market declines. The specific problem addressed in the study is the endowment losses experienced in fiscal year 2009 that affected the economic stability of United States' higher education in fiscal year 2010. The purpose of the quantitative correlation study was to measure the relationship between institutional characteristics and endowment investment performance in institutions of higher education in the United States, following the dramatic endowment monetary losses in and since the fiscal year ending in 2009. Endowment investment performance was measured against the independent variables of institutional characteristics (control, institutional type, governing bodies, religious affiliation, geographic location, tuition levels, student enrollment, selectivity, tuition discounting through institutional aid) and endowment characteristics (endowment size, contributions, and the percentage of total endowment designated as permanent endowment). Analysis of the endowment performance and institutional and endowment characteristics of 724 institutions included using Microsoft Excel and Statistical Package for Social Sciences (SPSS) to measure the relationships between variables. Secondary data were the basis for the correlation analysis in the study. Spearman's correlation coefficient and multiple regression analysis were applied to study the data.

The 2012 Beattie Study functions as an example of quantitative correlation research applied to higher education finance. The quantitative study used narrow research questions, hypotheses, and statistical tests to examine the financial crisis of 2008 and 2009 on higher education endowment investment performance. In conclusion, *A Quantitative Correlation Study: Institutional Characteristics and Endowment Investment Performance Following the 2008 – 2009 Financial Crisis* broadened the body of knowledge of endowments and higher education finance by measuring the relationship between institutional and endowment characteristics and endowment investment performance.

References

Altbach, P. G., Reisberg, L., & Rumbley, L. (2009). *Trends in global higher education: Tracking an academic revolution.* A report prepared for the UNESCO 2009 World Conference on Higher Education. Paris, France: UNESCO.

Chabotar, K. J. (2010). What about the rest of us? Small colleges in financial crisis. *Change, 42*(4), 6-13. Retrieved from http://www.changemag.org/

Cooper, D. R., & Schindler, P. (2011). *Business research methods* (11th ed.). New York, NY: McGraw-Hill.

Creswell, J. W. (2008). *Educational research: Planning, conducting, and evaluating quantitative and qualitative research* (3rd ed.). Upper Saddle River, NJ: Pearson.

Creswell, J. W. (2012). *Educational research: Planning, conducting, and evaluating quantitative and qualitative research* (4th ed.). Upper Saddle River, NJ: Pearson.

Doyle, W. R., & Delaney, J. A. (2009). Higher education: The new normal. *Change, 41*(4), 60. Retrieved from http://www.changemag.org/

Eckel, P., & Kezar, A. (2003). *Taking the reins: Institutional transformation in higher education.* Westport, CT: American Council on Education and Praeger Publishers.

Firestone, W. (1987). Meaning in method: The rhetoric of quantitative and qualitative research. *Educational Researcher, 16*(7), 16-21. doi:10.3102/0013189X016007016

Guidestar. (2011). IRS and financial documentation. Retrieved from http://www.guidestar.org

Humphreys, J. (2010). *Educational endowment and the financial crisis: Social costs and systemic risks in the shadow banking system.* Boston, MA: Center for Social Philanthropy–Tellus Institution.

Karmin, C., & Hechinger, J. (2008, October 17). *Crisis shakes the foundations of the ivory tower.* Retrieved from http://www.online.wsj.com

Larson, R., & Farber, B. (2006). *Elementary statistics: Picturing the world* (3rd ed.). Upper Saddle River, NJ: Pearson Prentice Hall.

National Association of College and University Business Officers-Commonfund 2010 Study of Endowments (NCSE). (2011a). Retrieved from http://www.nacubo.org

Neuman, W. L. (2006). *Social research methods: Qualitative and quantitative approaches.* Boston, MA: Allyn & Bacon.

Rea, L. M., & Parker, R. A. (2005). *Designing & conducting survey research: A comprehensive guide* (3rd ed.). San Francisco, CA: John Wiley & Sons.

Swenson, D. (2009). *Pioneering portfolio management: An unconventional approach to institutional investment.* New York, NY: Simon & Schuster.

Vogt, W. P. (2007). *Quantitative research methods for professionals.* Boston, MA: Allyn & Bacon.

Yeager, J. L., Nelson, G. M., Potter, E. A., Weidman, J. C., & Zullo, T. G. (2001). *ASHE reader on finance in higher education* (2nd ed.). Boston, MA: Pearson Custom Publishing.

About the Author...

Dr. Ellen Nicole Beattie resides in Baltimore, Maryland. Dr. Ellen holds several accredited degrees; a Bachelor of Arts (BA) in Economics from the College of Wooster; a Master of Organizational Management (MA) from University of Phoenix; a Master of Education– Curriculum and Instruction (MAEd) from University of Phoenix; and a Doctorate of Philosophy in Higher Education Administration (Ph.D.) from University of Phoenix – School of Advanced Studies.

Dr. Ellen holds faculty positions at Ashford University, Community College of Baltimore County, University of Phoenix, and University of the Rockies where she teaches graduate and undergraduate business, management, education, and ethics courses. She has received numerous awards for her commitment to academic excellence within the classroom. She is a peer reviewer for the Multimedia Educational Resource for Learning and Online Teaching (MERLOT).

Dr. Ellen has an extensive background in education administration, holding leadership positions in student services and operations. Her doctoral study, *A Quantitative Correlation Study: Institutional Characteristics and Endowment Investment Performance Following the 2008-2009 Financial Crisis*, provided her the opportunity to align her professional background in higher education with her love of the financial markets. Her research interest in financial literacy encouraged her to develop training materials and workshop curriculum aimed at increasing financial literacy among young women.

To reach Dr. Ellen Nicole Beattie for information on endowment research, higher education administration, or financial literacy, please e-mail: dr.ellenbeattie@gmail.com

CHAPTER 2

Refractive Thinking and the Influence of Religion and Religiosity on Leadership Practices

By Dr. Joseph Hage

Leadership is a relationship between those who aspire to lead and those who choose to follow.

James M. Kouzes & Barry Z. Posner

Religion is an institution often characterized as a unified system of beliefs combining various creeds, theologies, and doctrines about people's current and eternal destiny, as well as people's relationships with themselves and others around them including friends, enemies, and God (Durkheim, 1912; King, 2000; Spencer, 1862). In contrast, religiosity is a measure of religious knowledge, faith, fundamentalism, belief, piousness, orthodoxy, religiousness, holiness, and devotion of individuals and the extent to which they live and use religion for their own ends (Holdcroft, 2006). Since the early 1900s, thousands of leadership-related studies, articles, and books have been published around the world. Jogulu and Wood (2008) questioned the universality of Western leadership models, theories, and research, and cautioned against generalizing findings in a cross-cultural context because different cultures exhibit varying leadership practices and management styles (Jogulu, 2010; Zagorsek, Jaklic, & Stough, 2004). The Hage (2013) study was conducted to examine the relationship between religion, religiosity, and leadership practices among Christian and Muslim organizational leaders in Lebanon. This chapter includes an overview of the problem under investigation, the purpose of the study, a summary of the literature review, and a focused review of the research method and design along with a discussion of the survey instruments. This chapter concludes with the data analysis, findings, interpretations, conclusion, and implications of the study with a summary of lessons learned.

Tannenbaum and Schmidt (1958) asserted that effective leaders are those who accurately assess the forces significant to determining the appropriate behavior at any given time. Leaders have a major influence on organizational culture, shaping the performance of those they lead in the workplace. Some researchers concluded that religious beliefs shape the personality, behavior, ethical sensitivity, moral character, and value systems of individuals to varying degrees (Amine, 1996; Fernando & Jackson, 2006; Hunt & Vitell, 1986, 1993; King, Bell, & Lawrence, 2009; Pekerti & Sendjaya, 2010). Sauser (2005) posited in particular that people's behavior in daily life and work must conform to their religious beliefs. Although religious beliefs are integral to people's daily life experiences, faith and religion are often avoided in the workplace (King, Stewart, & McKay, 2010; Kutcher, Bragger, Rodriguez-Srednicki, & Masco, 2010). The Hage (2013) study focused on the extent of the relationship between religion and religiosity of organizational leaders and their leadership practices generally, and specifically in the context of non-Western Christian and non-Christian leaders. The focus of this chapter will be on the method and design of the study with lessons learned that may benefit future researchers.

Religion and Religiosity Matter

Organizational behavior is one factor that contributes to organizational effectiveness, leadership practices, followership, and organizational culture (Savage-Austin & Honeycutt, 2011). One's behavior is a product of family, religion, culture, society, and country. When leadership styles, religions, and business goals converge in an organizational environment, unique and varying dynamics come into play. Religion and values are an integral part of business life (Culliton, 1949; Gebert, Boerner, & Chatterjee, 2011); in which these entities play a major role in shaping individual traits (McCleary & Barro, 2006). Cultural norms often dictate the acceptable forms of leader behavior within the societal laws and acceptable norms.

Although Western societies have significant research about leadership, there is a paucity of literature about leadership in Middle Eastern cultures. Marcoulides, Yavas, Bilgin, and Gibson (1998) found that participative and autocratic styles were the major differentiators among business managers in the United States and Turkey, respectively. Hofstede (1980) asserted that the United States is an individualistic culture whereas Turkey and Iran are collectivist cultures. Yeganeh and Su (2007) and Sebhatu (1995) found similar results in the research of the culture's consequences on the leadership behaviors, attitudes, and styles of business leaders in Iran and Saudi Arabia. Ayyash-Abdo (2001) concluded that in Lebanon, the orientation of Christians was less collectivistic and trended toward more individualistic characteristics compared to their Muslim counterparts. Scandura and Dorfman (2004) asserted that Islam is fundamental to understanding leadership concepts in the Arab world.

Scholars suggested that religion has had a significant influence on leadership development (Modaff, Butler, & DeWine, 2012), on organizational leadership and management (Fernando & Jackson, 2006; Kriger & Seng, 2005), and on religion as an integral part of Arab culture (Amer, Hovey, Fox, & Rezcallah, 2008). Challenges may arise when employees from different cultures work together through activities like outsourcing, mergers, and acquisitions when organizational leaders face conflicting expectations of acceptable leadership practices (Chrobot-Mason, Ruderman, Weber, Ohlott, & Dalton, 2007). Studying conflict management styles among Christians and Muslim in France, Germany, and the United Kingdom, Croucher (2011) found that religion was a major contributor to the preference of handling conflict with Christians showing a preference for a dominating style and Muslims preferring the obliging and compromising conflict styles.

The Problem

The general problem Hage (2013) focused on is that published leadership studies are biased toward the leadership and followership approaches used in Western cultures such as the United States and Europe (Yeganeh & Su, 2007). Fernando and Jackson (2006) found in their research that religion had a significant effect on influencing the critical thinking and decision-making processes of business leaders. Even political leaders take religious factors into consideration when setting public policy.

The specific problem was that non-Western cultures have significant leadership and followership problems complicated by leadership practices. The events of the Arab Spring of 2011 unraveled as the world watched the rise of a populace revolting against political leadership and demanding democratic rule (Karam, 2011; Lynch, 2011). The results of the Arab uprising witnessed in the streets of Arab cities are testament to failed leader-follower exchanges. In some cases, these uprisings had a religious fervor element to them. Consequently, the influence of religion on leadership styles, practices, and perceptions in the workplace in plural countries must be investigated (Jogulu & Wood, 2008).

Lebanon is a small country in the Mediterranean where more than 20 Christian and Muslim religious sects often coexist in peace, but can on occasion confront each other in civil wars and conflicts. Religion and religiosity are important parts of Lebanese society (Chaaya, Sibai, Fayad, & El-Roueiheb, 2007), in which the country is structured along religious lines (Jawad, 2002). Lebanon is unique among Arab countries with a sizeable Christian population. Research indicated that, unlike other Arab countries, 83% of the Lebanese agree that men of religion should have influence over governmental decisions, but 83% believed that religious practice was a private issue to be separate from economic and social life (Tessler, 2010).

Searching Beyond the Traditional Limits of Leadership Styles

To examine the existence and extent of the relationship among religion, religiosity, and the leadership practices of organizational leaders in the workplace, the Hage (2013) study was conducted to seek answers beyond the traditional realm of the various leadership styles studied by many before. Religion is considered the foundation on which many social structures are built and has been an important element of societies for centuries. Debates have been ongoing about whether leadership style moderates spirituality or vice versa. Religion is more of a social membership whereas religiosity is grounded in spirituality and the living of a particular religion's precepts (Holdcroft, 2006). Many studies determined that culture has made a difference on leadership styles. Hage (2013) contributed to the discourse by focusing on religion and religiosity and how each may influence leadership practices in the workplace. As the research questions focused on the influence of religion and religiosity on leadership practices, it became clear that religion (independent nominal variable) and religiosity (independent ordinal variable) could affect leadership practices (dependent ordinal variables).

Conceptual Framework

The conceptual framework of this study centered on the Kouzes and Posner leadership practices model for exemplary leadership, an integrative theoretical framework of leadership challenges focusing on responsibility and performance and anchored on five dimensions of leadership practices (Kouzes & Posner, 1988, 1997, 2012). *Model the way* is about leading by example and walking the talk, which are key behaviors for successful leadership practices. *Inspire a shared vision* is an important leadership quality with an ability to communicate clearly to employees in the workplace (Schuttler, 2010). *Challenge the process* is how effective leaders become change agents who refuse to be restrained to the status quo and strive to innovate by pioneering in their field. *Enable others to act* is how successful leaders empower their followers to make decisions and act without fear of reprisals if those followers commit mistakes. *Encourage the heart* is important because people are led and humans have emotions and a social desire to be appreciated for their abilities, talents, skills, and performance (Johnson & Johnson, 2009).

Determining the Research Method and Design

Both qualitative and quantitative methods were considered for the study. The quantitative research paradigm is based on testing specific hypotheses, isolating and controlling variables, collecting numerical data, analyzing the data with statistical tools, and drawing conclusions from the results (Leedy & Ormrod, 2010). In contrast, qualitative research is based on the collection and analysis of non-numerical data such as collections of descriptions, pictures, qualities, and language (Steinberg, 2011).

The purpose of the Hage (2013) quantitative correlation study was to identify and measure the relationship between a leader's self-reported religion and religiosity (independent variables) and leadership practices (dependent variables) in the context of non-Western Christian and non-Christian organizational leaders in Lebanon, using hypothesis testing. Correlation studies are designed to investigate relationships among variables, but do not prove causation regardless of the strength of the correlation coefficient among the variables (Cooper & Schindler, 2011). Consequently, even if a correlation is the result of a reliable survey instrument, the correlation should not be considered as reliable proof of religion and religiosity influence over leadership practices in the workplace. Although multiple factors may be influencing the leadership practices, the limited aim of this study was to focus on the independent variables religion and religiosity.

The research was conducted to examine the religion and religiosity variables to predict organizational leadership practices. Descriptive quantitative research is more formulaic and refers to hypotheses and variables, thus reducing the possibility of researcher bias, as compared to qualitative research (Leedy & Ormrod, 2010). Quantitative research constitutes a popular research method in the social sciences and involves testing one or more hypotheses. In fact, quantitative research is based on a pre-specified method whereas qualitative research is recursive and results can be unclear (Willis, 2007).

Statistical analyses were used in the Hage (2013) study to investigate the hypothesized relationship between the variables. The results were somewhat mixed, supporting some prior studies and contradicting others. Differences in the hypothesized relationship between the religiosity and leadership practices of organizational leaders were noted. The outcomes of the Hage (2013) study indicated the existence of a significant relationship between religion and the five leadership dimensions (transformational leadership) whereas an insignificant relationship was found between religiosity and the five leadership dimensions (transformational leadership). The findings revealed that religion and religiosity and their influence on the behavior and practices of organizational leaders must be taken into account. For example, the religiosity and leadership practices of Christian organizational leaders aged 31 to 40 had a *Spearman's rho* (r_s) correlation coefficient of .59 (p = .000). The religiosity and leadership practices of Christian organizational leaders aged 41 to 50 had a *Spearman's rho* (r_s) correlation coefficient of .32 (p = .028). The correlation coefficients were considered small but significant for p < .05. However, the religiosity and leadership practices of Muslim respondents of all ages were not found to be significantly correlated.

Quantitative research is appropriate because this type of research follows a non-linear path in a natural setting (Neuman, 2011). Data presented in the form of numbers enable precise measurement. The quantitative correlation design is applicable when combinations of the independent predictor variables foretell the dependent criteria variables (Neuman, 2011). Correlations, however, do not imply a causation between the variables; hence, one cannot prove that specific leadership practices are the result of a particular religion or a certain level of religiosity (Duckworth, Tsukayama, & May, 2010; Leedy & Ormrod, 2010; Steinberg, 2011). A qualitative study would not have addressed the study's purpose adequately. Results of qualitative research cannot be generalized to larger populations. The quantitative method for the Hage (2013) study was appropriate to fulfill the purpose of the research, which was to investigate the relationship among the religion, religiosity, and leadership practices of organizational leaders.

Survey Instruments

Once the decision was reached to use the quantitative research method, determining the measurement instruments became a priority. Religion is a nominal variable that is easily captured in a questionnaire as part of demographic data. Religiosity and leadership practices needed to be measured using reliable and proven instruments that have been validated by researchers in prior studies. Reliable and validated survey instruments do add value and credibility to a study. Some researchers tend to reinvent the wheel by creating brand new survey instruments. By doing so, one runs the risk of constructing and using instruments that may invalidate the entire research process. Such risk includes delays in the data collection phase, repeated iterations of pilot studies, and even potentially getting the entire study rejected by the Institutional Review Board, after its completion.

The Hage (2013) study involved capturing demographic data and using two survey instruments. The Leadership Practices Inventory (LPI) questionnaire was used to measure the leadership practices of organizational leaders along five dimensions of leadership (Kouzes & Posner, 1997). The LPI has 30 leadership behaviors with six in each leadership practice. Respondents indicate how frequently they engage in the behavior using a 10-point Likert-type scale. Since 2000, I have had firsthand experience with the LPI as a frequent participant in studies conducted by one of its co-authors, Dr. Barry Posner, who was my leadership professor and dean of the Leavey School of Business at Santa Clara University, during my MBA studies there.

The LPI has been used in more than 70 countries, and validated across a wide variety of organizations, industries, and disciplines (Anand & UdayaSuriyan, 2010; Lam, 1998; Posner, 2011; Pugh, Fillingim, Blackbourn, Bunch, & Thomas, 2011). A pilot test of the LPI, involving 35 participants, revealed internal reliabilities above .70; which is considered quite acceptable (Salkind, 2003). Internal reliability coefficients for the five leadership subscales in this study, using Cronbach alpha, were Model (.88), Inspire (.93), Challenge (.93), Enable (.89), and Encourage (.95). An Overall Leadership scale was calculated as the sum of all five practices, and the coefficient alpha for this measure was .83.

The process of identifying the second survey instrument that measures religiosity was not as quick. After months of reviewing the literature, the Universal Religious Personality Inventory (URPI) instrument was identified. The URPI instrument uses a 5-point Likert-type scale to measure the self-reported level of religiosity of organizational leaders. Contact was initiated with Dr. Fazilah Idris, a Malaysian scholar who created the URPI. Idris granted permission to use the URPI survey or derive another survey from it.

To increase the response rate to the surveys for the Hage (2013) study, the Religiosity Practices Inventory (RPI) was derived to measure the leader's self-reported level of religiosity, which was used to compute a summative combined RPI Index. The RPI is a 60-item subset of the original 99-item URPI questionnaire. Participants were asked to indicate on the survey their religious affiliation, e.g. Christian or Muslim. Participants were asked for some additional demographic information such as age and gender. Non-parametric statistical tests were computed because the variables are nominal and ordinal. This study involved the collection of independent samples for two different religions, i.e. Christianity and Islam. Consequently, the appropriate significance test for two independent samples is the *t*-test (Weiers, 2005). The *t*-test was used to analyze the effect of one factor, religiosity, on the leadership practices dependent variables provided the samples were randomly chosen from normal populations that had equal variances (Cooper & Schindler, 2011). For religion, a nominal variable, the Chi-square (X^2) test was performed. Chi-square can be used on nominal and ordinal data as a measure of association in descriptive statistics or in inferential statistics (Neuman, 2011).

Population and Sampling

The population for this study was drawn from working adults (1.34 million) in Lebanon (Byblos Bank, 2011). One organizational leader was assumed for each four followers (N = 268000) spread among two major religions, Islam (60%) and Christianity (40%). Given the large size of the population and the impossibility of including all its elements in the study, sampling was necessary. Sampling is the selection process of a representative subset of a population to determine behaviors and characteristics about the entire population (Cooper & Schindler, 2011).

Researchers use samples to reach conclusions about the population without examining the entire population. Despite the misconception that the sample size must be a certain percentage of the population, the calculation of sample size is independent of the population size and determined in the same method regardless of the size of the population (Aaker, Kumar, & Day, 2007). The sample size (n = 384) was computed using two different formulas (Bartlett, Kotrlik, & Higgins, 2001; Krejecie & Morgan, 1970), consisting of 150 Christians (39.1%) and 234 Muslims (60.9%).

Pilot Testing and Data Collection

Pilot testing is recommended to reveal errors in the design or problems with the instruments (Cooper & Schindler, 2011). A convenience sample consisting of 44 individuals was identified to participate in the pilot study and 35 complete responses were submitted. Cronbach's alpha (α) is a measurement coefficient to determine the reliability of results by measuring the degree to which survey questions are homogeneous and reflective of the same underlying theories (Cooper & Schindler, 2011).

Survey questions with the α-value of .70 or higher were deemed reliable because they would correlate with overall questions across all participants (Salkind, 2003). The 35 pilot participants responded to the complete URPI survey and items were eliminated based upon scale construction methods using reduction in internal reliability as the elimination criteria. The subsequent derivative measure, labeled Religiosity Practices Index (RPI), had a Cronbach alpha of .83 (.79 for Muslim respondents and .86 for Christian respondents). As a result, both the LPI and the RPI were considered instruments psychometrically sound for the purpose of this study.

Subsequent to the pilot tests, invitations to participate in the study were e-mailed to 9,500 randomly selected people from a subscription-only directory of organizations in Lebanon. Some of the targeted organizational leaders opted out of the study. Others expressed concerns regarding the purpose of inquiring about religion and religiosity, especially that Lebanon had suffered through many decades of civil war and religious strife. Reminders were sent at 7-day intervals automatically by the LimeSurvey tool. Some respondents indicated a preference for completing paper-based surveys.

During the 18-week data collection period, 448 responses were received. Data were collected past the quota level to increase randomness and were reduced in number to the quota level via a random selection process. When dealing with a large sample, one must anticipate a longer data collection phase. The RPI included five lie detection questions, which may disqualify and exclude a participant from the study. Thus, casting a wider net was necessary to increase the number of respondents beyond the desired 384 target.

Validity and Reliability

Researchers basing their studies on measurement must be concerned with the reliability, dependability, and accuracy of measurement (Cronbach, 1951). If the tools used in data collection and analysis are invalid or unreliable, the results would be inconclusive (Salkind, 2011). The survey instruments used were not unique to this study. The URPI and the LPI surveys have been already validated through numerous types of validity such as content validity, criterion validity, and construct validity (Barber & Korbanka, 2003). Content validity may be established by determining the extent to which the surveys are providing adequate coverage of the research questions guiding this study (Cooper & Schindler, 2011). The LPI is a validated instrument (Anand & UdayaSuriyan, 2010; Pugh et al., 2011). Posner (2011) reported that LPI survey participants have been spread geographically among the United States (79%) and more than 100 countries (21%). Posner (2010a) reported internal reliability coefficients on the LPI-Self ranging from .68 to .79.

The power of a statistical test is the probability that the null hypothesis will be rejected even if when the null hypothesis is false and should be rejected (Faul, Erdfelder, Lang, & Buchner, 2007). Post hoc analysis computes the statistical power 1-β as a function of significance level α, sample size, and population effect size (Faul, Erdfelder, Buchner, & Lang, 2009). A power of .80

is a convention proposed for general use in behavioral sciences (Cohen, 1992), while some researchers argue for a higher power level of .85 to .90 (Lenth, 2001). A power analysis was conducted using a linear multiple regression random model statistical test to assess and demonstrate the sufficiency of the sample size by using the G*Power 3 statistical power calculator. The result of the power analysis was .95 thus concluding that the sample size is adequate for this study.

Data Analysis, Findings, and Interpretations

Microsoft Excel and IBM SPSS were used for statistical analyses. The Hage (2013) study involved the collection of independent samples for two different religions, i.e. Christianity and Islam. In the study, four research questions were addressed.

RQ1: To what extent are the leadership practices of organizational leaders based on their religion?

H1$_0$: There are no significant differences in the leadership practices of organizational leaders based on their religion.

The descriptive statistics for mean (M) and standard deviation (SD) showed that Christian organizational leaders exhibited transformational leadership behavior in scoring higher than the median in all five categories of leadership practices (Fields & Herold, 1997; Posner, 2010b). Muslim respondents tended to be more autocratic in their leadership style as they scored lower than the median in all five dimensions of leadership practices. Yeganeh and Su (2008), Hofstede, Hofstede, and Minkov (2010), Abdalla and Al-Homoud (2001), and Jogulu (2010) reached similar conclusions in their research. Members of the Muslim cluster of the sample exhibited the highest level of devotion in practicing their religion and the null hypothesis (H1$_0$) was rejected.

RQ2: What correlation, if any, exists among the religiosity of organizational leaders and their leadership practices?

H2$_0$: No significant correlation exists among the religiosity of organizational leaders and their leadership practices.

Correlations between the RPI Index and each of the leadership practice dimensions were computed for the entire sample showing a small negative correlation with r_s values ranging between -.02 and -.08. A small but statistically significant correlation was measured between the religiosity level and leadership practices of Christian organizational leaders. In contrast, for the Muslim group, no significant correlation was found. Based on these findings, the results for the second hypothesis were mixed. This is important because the findings indicate that the stronger the religiosity levels, the less transformational leaders become. The null hypothesis for Christian respondents (H2$_0$) was rejected, but not for Muslim organizational leaders.

RQ3: To what extent do religiosity and religion predict leadership practices in the workplace?

H3$_0$: Religiosity is a more significant predictor of leadership practices than religion in the workplace.

A multiple regression analysis was performed with the LPI Score as the dependent variable and multiple predictor variables religion, religiosity, age group, type of organization, gender, number of people led, and size of organization. Regressing the LPI Score on religion and religiosity resulted in an R^2 statistic value of .210 (ΔR^2 = .008, p = .031) representing a 4% fluctuation. This increase was evidence that religiosity makes an incremental addition to understanding leadership practices. Consequently, $H3_0$ was rejected because results reflected that religion is a more significant predictor of leadership practices than religiosity.

RQ4: What differences, if any, existed in the leadership practices of organizational leaders from different religious backgrounds based on their religiosity?

$H4_0$: No differences exist in the leadership practices of organizational leaders from different religious backgrounds based on their religiosity.

This research question was intended to determine whether a leader's devotion to his or her religious faith is more influential over leadership practices than his or her religious affiliation is. Upon reviewing the median RPI Indices of the overall sample, it was evident that Muslim respondents exhibited the highest level of religiosity and devotion to their religious beliefs. To test the null hypothesis, a linear regression analysis was performed for each of the five leadership practice dimensions and the aggregate LPI Score on religiosity for each religion.

For both Christian and Muslim organizational leaders, not much of their overall leadership practices score could be explained by religiosity. For Christians, religiosity explained approximately 6% of their LPI Score, which was statistically significant, and for Muslims, it was less than 1%. The analysis of the mean RPI Indices and LPI Scores and the regression results led to the mixed conclusions by rejecting $H4_0$ for Christians and failing to reject $H4_0$ for Muslims.

Conclusion and Implications

Hage (2013) adds empirical evidence that there is a relationship between religion and leadership practices in the workplace. Several implications emanate from these results. The study supports assertions by Metcalfe (2007) and Tayeb (1997) that for Muslims, religion is a significant influencer of economic, political, gender, and interpersonal relations in the workplace. The findings confirmed prior research that organizational leaders in collectivist cultures are likely to exhibit transformational leadership characteristics (Jogulu, 2010). The results are consistent with those showing that religion is a significant influencer of leadership development (Modaff et al., 2012) and that religion affects organizational leadership and management (Fernando & Jackson, 2006; Kriger & Seng, 2005).

Hage (2013) confirmed previous findings by Sengupta (2010) and Yaghi (2008) that religious beliefs affected leadership style and how leaders process information and make decisions in the workplace. The study may explain how the research conclusions apply to businesses and cultures in a global context. Hage (2013) supports prior research showing that religion is an integral part of Arab culture (Amer et al., 2008) and is consistent with conclusions by other scholars (Al-Khatib, Robertson, Stanton, & Vitell, 2002; Sidani & Thornberry, 2010; Wunderle, 2007) that a strong relationship exists between the religious convictions of Arab managers and how they interact with their subordinates.

The results affirmed the challenges detailed in the conceptual framework of the leadership practices model for exemplary leadership. One important inference is that, for this particular sample, higher levels of religiosity were inversely correlated with transformational leadership. Overall, the LPI Score for Muslims was indicative of a weaker transformational leadership style with a tendency toward an autocratic style. These findings are consistent with the generally more hierarchical and autocratic philosophy of Islam in comparison with Christianity. Results provide a construct for organizational leaders to help them better recognize their leadership style and assist them in identifying areas for improvements in their leadership practices.

Leadership is a mature field of study sustained by a vast collection of scholarly literature, but the field of leadership and its relation to religion and religiosity is quite immature. Results of the present study were somewhat mixed, supporting some prior studies and contradicting others. Hage (2013) confirmed that leadership practices were significantly complicated by religion and religiosity in a non-Western culture. With the major changes taking place in the Arab world and the religious influence on their outcomes, Hage (2013) shed some light on the effect of religion and religiosity on leadership styles, practices, and perceptions in the workplace in pluralistic countries.

Religion and religiosity are integral parts of culture and influence human behavior especially in the case of those individuals who have a high degree of religiosity (King et al., 2009). Religious beliefs influence the behavior of organizational leaders affecting employee morale, retention, and productivity (Morgan, 2004). Hage (2013) showed that focusing solely on cultural and social factors while ignoring the effects of religious beliefs on leadership practices in the workplace is an ill-advised strategy. Ongoing empirical examination of the relationship between religion and leadership practices in the workplace is an important endeavor to pursue.

Summary

Writing this chapter presented an opportunity to think back on the entire research process of the Hage (2013) study, an effort extended over a period of more than 2 years. I want to present readers and future researchers with some recommendations and lessons learned to be taken into consideration in impending studies. Here are the top 10 items to consider:

- Keep the number of research questions to a manageable number, 3 to 4 at most. One tends to want to find answers to too many questions, thus complicating the study and extending its completion time.

- Articulate the research questions and keep the null hypotheses and their corresponding statistical tests in mind.

- If at all feasible, avoid dealing with too many independent variables (3 independent variables at the most). Most important, keep the number of dependent variables to a minimum (just 1 dependent variable, if possible). Keep in mind that the types of variables used, e.g. nominal, ordinal, interval, or ratio, will determine the kinds of statistical tests to analyze and interpret the data.

- Avoid creating custom surveys for the study. Use existing instruments that have been validated and deemed reliable in prior research.

- Determine an adequate sample size that is a representative subset of the entire population and that enables the generalization of the findings to the entire population.

- Use post hoc analysis by computing the statistical power to assess and demonstrate the sufficiency of the sample size.

- Conduct the research with an open mind, without any preconceived notions, and keep personal biases in check.

- Never assume that qualitative studies are easier to conduct than quantitative studies. In most cases, interview answers in qualitative studies still need to be coded and analyzed with statistical tools.

- Do not be intimidated by large volumes of numbers. Simply rely on statistical analysis tools to transform the data into consumable information that can be interpreted.
- Formulating the research questions and hypotheses, and determining the statistical tests to be conducted are the hardest part of the study. The data collection and analysis phases should be stress-free and the most enjoyable part of the process.

Finally, I would hope that completing my dissertation has contributed to better understand the influences of religious affiliation and religiosity on leadership practices in a diverse workplace. Approaching such sensitive non-traditional topics enabled me to be a refractive thinker; one who pushes the envelope of knowledge, thinks beyond the norm, and inquires beyond the obvious.

References

Aaker, D. A., Kumar, V., & Day, G. S. (2007). Marketing research (9th ed.). Hoboken, NJ: John Wiley & Sons.

Abdalla, I. A., & Al-Homoud, M. A. (2001). Exploring the implicit leadership theory in the Arabian Gulf States. Applied Psychology: An International Review, 50, 503-531.

Al-Khatib, J. A., Robertson, C. J., D'Auria Stanton, A., & Vitell, S. J. (2002). Business ethics in the Arab Gulf States: A three-country study. [Study]. International Business Review, 11(1), 97-111. doi:10.1016/s0969-5931(01)00049-x

Amer, M. M., Hovey, J. D., Fox, C. M., & Rezcallah, A. (2008). Initial development of the Brief Arab Religious Coping Scale (BARCS). Journal of Muslim Mental Health, 3(1), 69-88. doi:10.1080/15564900802156676

Amine, L. S. (1996). The need for moral champions in global marketing. European Journal of Marketing, 30(5), 81-94. doi:10.1108/03090569610118795

Anand, R., & UdayaSuriyan, G. (2010). Emotional intelligence and its relationship with leadership practices. International Journal of Business & Management, 5(2), 65-76.

Ayyash-Abdo, H. (2001). Individualism and collectivism: The case of Lebanon. Social Behavior and Personality, 29, 503-518. doi:10.2224/sbp.2001.29.5.503

Barber, A., & Korbanka, J. (2003). Research and statistics for the social sciences. Boston, MA: Pearson Education.

Bartlett, J. E., II, Kotrlik, J. W., & Higgins, C. C. (2001, Spring). Organizational research: Determining appropriate sample size in survey research. Information Technology, Learning, and Performance Journal, 19(1).

Byblos Bank. (2011). Lebanon this week. (Vol. February 28-March 5, 2011). Beirut, Lebanon: Byblos Bank SAL -Economic Research & Analysis Department.

Chaaya, M., Sibai, A. M., Fayad, R., & El-Roueiheb, Z. (2007). Religiosity and depression in older people: Evidence from underprivileged refugee and non-refugee communities in Lebanon. Aging & Mental Health, 11(1), 37-44. doi:10.1080/13607860600735812

Chrobot-Mason, D., Ruderman, M. N., Weber, T. J., Ohlott, P. J., & Dalton, M. A. (2007). Illuminating a cross-cultural leadership challenge: When identity groups collide. International Journal of Human Resource Management, 18, 2011-2036. doi:10.1080/09585190701639778

Cohen, J. (1992). A power primer. Psychological Bulletin, 112(1), 155-159. doi:10.1037/0033-2909.112.1.155

Cooper, D. R., & Schindler, P. S. (2011). Business research methods (11th ed.). New York, NY: McGraw-Hill Irwin.

Cronbach, L. (1951). Coefficient alpha and the internal structure of tests. Psychometrika, 16(3), 297-334. doi:10.1007/bf02310555

Croucher, S. (2011). Muslim and Christian conflict styles in Western Europe. [Research Paper]. International Journal of Conflict Management, 22(1), 60-74. doi:10.1108/10444061111103625

Culliton, J. W. (1949, May). Business and religion. Harvard Business Review, 27(3), 265-271.

Duckworth, A. L., Tsukayama, E., & May, H. (2010). Establishing causality using longitudinal hierarchical linear modeling: An illustration predicting achievement from self-control. Social Psychological and Personality Science, 1, 311-317. doi:10.1177/1948550609359707

Durkheim, E. (1912). The elementary forms of religious life (C. Cosman, Trans.). Oxford, UK: Oxford University Press.

Faul, F., Erdfelder, E., Buchner, A., & Lang, A.-G. (2009). Statistical power analyses using G*Power 3.1: Tests for correlation and regression analyses. Behavior Research Methods, 41, 1149-1160. doi:10.3758/BRM.41.4.1149

Faul, F., Erdfelder, E., Lang, A.-G., & Buchner, A. (2007). G*Power 3: A flexible statistical power analysis program for the social, behavioral, and biomedical sciences. Behavior Research Methods, 39(2), 175-191.

Fernando, M., & Jackson, B. (2006, June). The influence of religion-based workplace spirituality on business leaders' decision-making: An inter-faith study. Journal of Management and Organization, 12(1), 23-39.

Fields, D. L., & Herold, D. M. (1997). Using the Leadership Practices Inventory to measure transformational and transactional leadership. Educational and Psychological Measurement, 57, 569-579. doi:10.1177/0013164497057004003

Gebert, D., Boerner, S., & Chatterjee, D. (2011). Do religious differences matter? An analysis in India. Team Performance Management, 17(3), 224-240.

Hage, J. (2013). Influence of religion and religiosity on leadership practices in the workplace: A quantitative correlation study (Unpublished doctoral dissertation). University of Phoenix, Arizona, United States.

Hofstede, G. (1980). Culture's consequences: International differences in work-related values (Vol. 5). Thousand Oaks, CA: Sage.

Hofstede, G., Hofstede, G. J., & Minkov, M. (2010). Cultures and organizations: Software of the mind - Intercultural cooperation and its importance for survival (3rd ed.). New York, NY: McGraw-Hill.

Holdcroft, B. B. (2006). What is religiosity? Catholic Education: A Journal of Inquiry & Practice, 10(1), 89-103.

Hunt, S. D., & Vitell, S. J. (1986). A general theory of marketing ethics: A retrospective and revision. Journal of Macromarketing, 6(1), 5-16.

Hunt, S. D., & Vitell, S. J. (1993). The general theory of marketing ethics: a retrospective and revision. In N. C. Smith & J. A. Quelch (Eds.), Ethics in marketing (pp. 775-801). Homewood, IL: Irwin.

Jawad, R. (2002). A profile of social welfare in Lebanon. Global Social Policy, 2, 319-342. doi:10.1177/1468018102002003050

Jogulu, U. D. (2010). Culturally-linked leadership styles. Leadership & Organization Development Journal, 31 705-719. doi:10.1108/01437731011094766

Jogulu, U. D., & Wood, G. J. (2008). A cross-cultural study into peer evaluations of women's leadership effectiveness. [Research Paper]. Leadership & Organization Development Journal, 29, 600-616. doi:10.1108/01437730810906344

Johnson, D. W., & Johnson, F. P. (2009). Joining together: Group theory and group skills (10th ed.). Boston, MA: Pearson Education.

Karam, C. M. (2011). Good organizational soldiers: Conflict-related stress predicts citizenship behavior. [Research Paper]. International Journal of Conflict Management, 22(3), 300-319. doi:10.1108/10444061111152982

King, J. E., Jr., Bell, M. P., & Lawrence, E. (2009). Religion as an aspect of workplace diversity: An examination of the U.S. context and a call for international research. Journal of Management, Spirituality & Religion, 6(1), 43-57. doi:10.1080/14766080802648631

King, J. E., Jr., Stewart, M. M., & McKay, P. F. (2010). Religiosity, religious identity, and bias towards workplace others. Academy of Management Annual Meeting Proceedings, 1-6. doi:10.5465/ambpp.2010.54492059

King, S. M. (2000). Toward a new administrative ethic: An understanding and application of the Judeo-Christian tradition to administrative issues. Public Integrity 2(1), 17–28.

Kouzes, J. M., & Posner, B. Z. (1988). The leadership challenge San Francisco, CA: Jossey-Bass.

Kouzes, J. M., & Posner, B. Z. (1997). Leadership Practices Inventory [LPI], Participant's Workbook Supplement (2nd ed.). San Francisco, CA: Jossey-Bass Pfeiffer.

Kouzes, J. M., & Posner, B. Z. (2012). The leadership challenge (5th ed.). San Francisco, CA: John Wiley & Sons.

Krejecie, R. V., & Morgan, D. W. (1970). Determining sample size for research activities. Educational and Psychological Measurement, 30, 607-610.

Kriger, M., & Seng, Y. (2005). Leadership with inner meaning: A contingency theory of leadership based on the worldviews of five religions. The Leadership Quarterly, 16, 771-806. doi:10.1016/j.leaqua.2005.07.007

Kutcher, E., Bragger, J., Rodriguez-Srednicki, O., & Masco, J. (2010). The role of religiosity in stress, job attitudes, and organizational citizenship behavior. Journal of Business Ethics, 95, 319-337. doi:10.1007/s10551-009-0362-z

Lam, S. S. K. (1998). An assessment of the reliability and validity of the Leadership Practices Inventory in Hong Kong. International Journal of Management, 15(1), 57-59.

Leedy, P. D., & Ormrod, J. E. (2010). Practical research: Planning and design (9th ed.). Saddle River, NJ: Pearson Education.

Lenth, R. V. (2001). Some practical guidelines for effective sample size determination. The American Statistician, 55(3), 187-193.

Lynch, B. (2011, Nov-Dec). Arab Spring: Origins, implications, outlook. [Proceeding]. New Zealand International Review, 36(6), 9-12.

Marcoulides, G. A., Yavas, B. F., Bilgin, Z., & Gibson, C. B. (1998). Reconciling culturalist and rationalist approaches: Leadership in the United States and Turkey. Thunderbird International Business Review, 40, 563-583.

McCleary, R. M., & Barro, R. J. (2006, Spring). Religion and economy. Journal of Economic Perspectives, 20(2), 49-72.

Metcalfe, B. D. (2007). Gender and human resource management in the Middle East. International Journal of Human Resource Management, 18(1), 54-74. doi:10.1080/09585190601068292

Modaff, D. P., Butler, J. A., & DeWine, S. (2012). Organizational communication: Foundations, challenges, and misunderstandings (3rd ed.). Glenview, IL: Pearson Education.

Morgan, J. F. (2004). How should business respond to a more religious workplace? SAM Advanced Management Journal (07497075), 69(4), 11-19.

Neuman, W. L. (2011). Social research methods: Qualitative and quantitative approaches (7th ed.). Boston, MA: Pearson Education.

Pekerti, A. A., & Sendjaya, S. (2010). Exploring servant leadership across cultures: Comparative study in Australia and Indonesia. International Journal of Human Resource Management, 21, 754-780. doi:10.1080/09585191003658920

Posner, B. Z. (2010a, February). Psychometric properties of the student Leadership Practices Inventory,1-29. Retrieved from The Leadership Challenge website http://www.leadershipchallenge.com/Research-section-Our-Authors-Research-Detail/psychometric-properties-of-the-student-leadership-practices-inventory.aspx

Posner, B. Z. (2010b, September). Leadership Practices Inventory (LPI) data analysis, 1-45. from The Leadership Challenge website http://media.wiley.com/assets/2260/07/LPIDataAnalysisSept2010.pdf

Posner, B. Z. (2011, December). LPI Online normative database, 1-2. Retrieved from The Leadership Challenge website http://www.leadershipchallenge.com/Research-section-Our-Authors-Research-Detail/lpi-online-normative-database-december-2011.aspx

Pugh, A. G., Fillingim, J. G., Blackbourn, J. M., Bunch, D., & Thomas, C. (2011). Faculty validation of the Leadership Practices Inventory with secondary school principals. National Forum of Educational Administration & Supervision Journal, 28(3), 4-11.

Salkind, N. J. (2003). Exploring research (5th ed.). Upper Saddle River, NJ: Prentice Hall.

Salkind, N. J. (2011). Statistics for people who (think they) hate statistics (4th ed.). Upper Saddle River, NJ: Sage.

Sauser Jr., W. I. (2005). Ethics in business: Answering the call. Journal of Business Ethics, 58, 345-357. doi:10.1007/s10551-004-5715-z

Savage-Austin, A. R., & Honeycutt, A. (2011). Servant leadership: A phenomenological study of practices, experiences, organizational effectiveness, and barriers. Journal of Business & Economics Research, 9(1), 49-54.

Scandura, T., & Dorfman, P. (2004). Leadership research in an international and cross-cultural context. The Leadership Quarterly, 15, 277-307. doi:10.1016/j.leaqua.2004.02.004

Schuttler, R. (2010). The law of communication: Correlating performance to communication. In R. Schuttler (Ed.), Laws of communication: The intersection where leadership meets employee performance. Hoboken, NJ: Wiley.

Sebhatu, P. P. (1995). Culture's consequences on business leaders in the Middle East with a focus on Saudi Arabia. Journal of International Business Studies, 26, 915-916.

Sengupta, S. S. (2010). Correlates of spiritual orientation & managerial effectiveness. Indian Journal of Industrial Relations, 45(5), 45-60.

Sidani, Y., & Thornberry, J. (2010). The current Arab work ethic: Antecedents, implications, and potential remedies. Journal of Business Ethics, 91(1), 35-49. doi:10.1007/s10551-009-0066-4

Spencer, H. (1862). First principles. New York, NY: D. Appleton.

Steinberg, W. J. (2011). Statistics alive! (2nd ed.). Los Angeles, CA: Sage.

Tannenbaum, R., & Schmidt, W. H. (1958, March-April). How to choose a leadership pattern. Harvard Business Review, 36(2), 95-101.

Tayeb, M. (1997). Islamic revival in Asia and human resource management. Employee Relations, 19, 352-364.

Tessler, M. (2010). Religion, religiosity and the place of Islam in political life: Insights from the Arab barometer surveys. Middle Eastern Law & Governance, 2(2), 221-252. doi:10.1163/187633710x500748

Willis, J. W. (2007). Foundations of qualitative research: Interpretive and critical approaches. Thousand Oaks, CA: Sage.

Wunderle, W. D. (2007). Through the lens of cultural awareness: A primer for U.S. Armed Forces deploying to Arab and Middle Eastern countries. Fort Leavensworth, KS: U.S. Dept. of the Army, Combat Studies Institute Press.

Yaghi, A. (2008). Leadership values influencing decision-making; An examination of nine Islamic, Hindu, and Christian nonprofit institutions in the U.S. South Asian Journal of Management, 15(1), 24-41.

Yeganeh, H., & Su, Z. (2007). Comprehending core cultural orientations of Iranian managers. Cross Cultural Management: An International Journal, 14, 336-353. doi:10.1108/13527600710830359

Yeganeh, H., & Su, Z. (2008). An examination of human resource management practices in Iranian public sector. Personnel Review, 37(2), 203-221. doi:10.1108/00483480810850542

Zagorsek, H., Jaklic, M., & Stough, S. J. (2004). Comparing leadership practices between the United States, Nigeria, and Slovenia: Does culture matter? Cross Cultural Management, 11(2), 16-34.

About the Author...

Dr. Joe Hage holds a doctorate degree Summa Cum Laude in Business Administration from University of Phoenix, an M.B.A. Summa Cum Laude from Santa Clara University, and a B.S. in Electrical and Computer Engineering from Northeastern University. Dr. Joe's career spans more than 33 years in the information technology industry where he has held various positions in executive leadership, software development, project management, product management, consulting, sales, and marketing. Dr. Joe is Associate Chief Information Officer at the American University of Beirut (AUB), a leading provider of education and healthcare services in the Middle East.

Preceding AUB, Dr. Joe was Chief Executive Officer of eSharing, an information technology solutions company. Dr. Joe spent 9 years at Agile Software product lifecycle management and supply chain management solutions (acquired by Oracle) where he was Senior Vice President and General Manager of the Small and Medium Enterprise Solutions Division (2003-2006), Senior Vice President of Products and Technology (2001-2003), and Vice President of Corporate Marketing (1997-2000). Dr. Joe also held positions at Universant, Starfish Software (acquired by Motorola), Novell, Borland, Prime Computer, Data General, and Honeywell in the United States, Canada, Saudi Arabia, the United Arab Emirates, and Lebanon.

To reach Dr. Joe Hage,

Website: http://www.joe.me
E-mail: dr@joe.me
Twitter: http://twitter.com/DrJoeHage
LinkedIn: http://linkedin.com/in/joehage
Facebook: http://facebook.com/DrJoeHage

CHAPTER 3

Researching Close to Home: Using Refractive Thinking to Examine Professional Colleagues

By Dr. Ronald C. Jones & Dr. Cheryl A. Lentz

Examining the leadership behaviors of colleagues is a daunting leap of faith in the interest of higher learning. Jones (2013) completed the doctoral study entitled *Examining Leadership Styles and Financial Performance within Rural Electric Cooperatives* while serving as President and Chairperson of the Board of a rural electric cooperative and serving on the board of directors of an electric generation and transmission cooperative. Numerous participants were professional colleagues; all were general managers of rural electric cooperatives. By describing the research method, procedures, and problem-solving philosophy Jones used, other doctoral scholars may find practical solutions to meet the challenge and overcome the obstacles associated with research involving colleagues.

The initial process of doctoral research requires identifying a topic, oftentimes originating from a personal curiosity of an observed or experienced localized problem. The desire to study a personalized problem because of professional interest and possibly scholarly fascination could increase researcher motivation. At the same time, conducting research on the behaviors of colleagues offers the potential for problematic issues to diminish or destroy the integrity of the study. Validity threats exist because of the opinions, potential biases, and preconceived notions of the researcher regarding participants and behavior (Creswell, 2009). Ethical issues are present because of the possibility of conflicts-of-interest, the potential to inflict professional or emotional harm on the participants, or revealing information that could identify the participants. Exposing ineffective leadership behaviors or unproductive organizational practices along with inviting criticism from contemporaries could cause a doctoral scholar to forego research that included professional colleagues.

How does one overcome the obstacles to expose a problem close to home and conduct a study deemed worthy of doctoral research? The answer lies in selecting the appropriate method and design, along with incorporating proper structure and safeguards. Although grounded within the existing body of knowledge regarding the topic of study, oftentimes doctoral research requires critical thinking and acting beyond the scope of prior studies. Students must be willing to be pioneers to step out of their comfort zones and perceived boundaries. Replication of existing studies, procedures, and thought processes can result in worthwhile results, yet the process of refractive thinking allows the researcher to remove boundaries, obstacles, and rules to develop new knowledge regarding a professionally close problem.

Selecting the Appropriate Method

A research methodology is the guiding model from which to conduct research (Wahyuni, 2012). With quantitative, qualitative, and mixed methods research as options (Amitabh & Gupta, 2010), doctoral scholars often ponder regarding the appropriate methodology to conduct research on the identified problem. All three methods provide a conduit to doctoral success if properly managed and structured. Mixed methods research incorporates quantitative and qualitative methods to study a problem deemed to be of such magnitude that one research method would not be adequate to address the issue (Symonds & Gorard, 2010). Doctoral students might remove mixed methods research as an option because of the level of rigor and difficulty (Fielding, 2010). Qualitative data analysis relies on the researcher's interpretation of the data (Labaree, 2011). The qualitative researcher explores the phenomenon through interviews with participants closely associated with the problem under study. Qualitative researchers often use a smaller sample size than required in the quantitative method, yet conducting research as an *insider* might reduce the participants' willingness to share life experiences with a colleague. Aspects of the quantitative method include detached data collection through surveys, minimal data interpretation, and fact-based examination of the problem (Wahyuni, 2012). In the Jones' (2013) study, the problem was a lack of evidence regarding the effect of leadership style on the financial aspects of rural electric cooperatives. Jones faced the dilemma of selecting the appropriate method to study the problem without the elements of researcher bias and coercion regarding recruiting participants. After reflection, investigation, and accepting expert counsel from doctoral advisors, Jones selected the quantitative method to overcome the challenges associated with researching close to home. Quantitative methods studies are valuable to creating new knowledge and contributing to the existing body of knowledge with a high degree of credibility, reliability, and validity; all vital aspects of doctoral research (Labaree, 2011; Parab & Bhalerao, 2010).

Jones' (2013) doctoral committee members provided ample warnings regarding conflicts-of-interest, ethical dilemmas of using participants holding a professional affiliation, and attempting to collect data from organizational leaders. Although unknowns existed, the potential obstacles stimulated the desire to study the problem and provide relevant information to organizational leaders, possibly leading to improved business practices within the rural electric cooperative industry. With the industry chosen, a problem identified, and a research method selected, writing the proposal progressed, yet challenges remained ahead.

Examining the relationship between leadership style and electric rates was the original intent of the Jones' (2013) study. A committee member questioned the validity of the presented concept, claiming that with numerous factors influencing electric rates, revealing a significant correlation between leadership style and rates would be meaningless. Receiving approval of the proposal required changing the dependent variable of electric rates to financial performance, a variable in which organizational leaders directly influence. Changing the focus from electric rates to financial performance did not significantly alter the objective of the study because electric rates in rural electric cooperatives remain key performance indicators that reflect financial performance (National Rural Electric Cooperative Association [NRECA], 2012). Rural electric cooperatives operate under a federal mandate to base electric rates on total cost plus a margin to maintain financial viability (NRECA, 2012); therefore, the primary goal of the study remained intact. By using a non-confrontational style when investigating or proposing alternatives to keep communication channels with committee members open, refractive thinking preserved Jones' ability to remain interested and personally engaged regarding this topic. Refractive thinkers accept *no* as a means to develop another viable option, not the end of the pursuit of new knowledge.

When superiors of the doctoral process say *no*, the response need not be argumentative, but inquisitive, cooperative, and confident to move beyond the obstacle according to sound research principles and protocols. Doctoral programs consist of rules, policies, and nonnegotiable procedures. Successful doctoral students do not by-pass academic requirements or operate outside the structured boundaries, yet oftentimes success requires diligent curiosity, extensive questioning, exploration, and refractive thinking. Producing a previously unknown solution to overcome an obstacle might require stretching and bending existing boundaries in an effort to look toward doing what has not yet been done to add to the ever-expanding body of knowledge within one's field of study.

Reliability and Validity: Quantitative Research

Quantitative researchers focus on validity and reliability, facilitating replication by other researchers and generalization of the results to the total population (Wahyuni, 2012). Reliability is an essential prerequisite of validity (Brahma, 2009). In quantitative research, reliability refers to degree of consistency in the measures or instruments used to collect and analyze data, or the degree that the survey delivers consistent results if replicated by another researcher (Brahma, 2009; Wahyuni, 2012). Validity refers to the credibility of the data regarding the studied phenomenon, and transferability of the result to other organizations, industries, or regions (Wahyuni, 2012).

The geographic region of the Jones' (2013) study was the southern United States. Rural electric cooperatives exist in 47 states and numerous other countries, allowing other researchers ample replication opportunities in other regions of the country and world. By maintaining reliability and validity, Jones provided future doctoral scholars a quality foundation to replicate the study with confidence. The sample population of the Jones study consisted of 102 general managers of rural electric cooperatives, yet 864 rural electric cooperatives exist within the United States. Although the findings reflect the data collected from the sample population, upholding reliability and validity standards allowed the results to be generalized to 864 general managers. In other words, the 864 general managers within the total population are likely to reflect the same findings and correlations as the sample population.

Reliability

The primary reliability concern of a quantitative researcher is of the survey instrument. Jones (2013) used the Multifactor Leadership Questionnaire (MLQ) developed by Bass and Avolio (2004) to collect leadership style data. Recognizing that qualitative researchers use questionnaires and quantitative researchers use surveys, the word *questionnaire* in the title of the MLQ presented an obstacle to overcome. By researching prior use of the MLQ by numerous researchers, Jones provided within the study ample support that the MLQ was a survey, not a questionnaire. The MLQ is a reliable instrument to identify the leadership styles of transformational, transactional, and laissez-faire (Sadeghi & Pihie, 2012). Leong and Fischer (2011) studied the reliability of the MLQ across a variety of cultures, finding an adequate level of consistency to identify leadership styles. Using a survey with proven reliability regarding the identification of leadership styles, Jones avoided the problems associated with collecting data with an unreliable and inconsistent survey.

An existing, validated survey might not be available for collecting data needed regarding a particular variable. A quantitative researcher has the option to conduct a pilot study of a self-developed survey to establish reliability. Participants of the pilot study should be representative of the target population, yet excluded from the formal study as participants. Doctoral students should consider the time, effort, and resource-saving value of existing, proven survey. By aligning the variables with a validated survey, quantitative researchers eliminate additional steps and approvals within the doctoral program. Jones (2013) desired to study the relationship between leadership behaviors and financial performance. The challenge emanated from a means to measure leadership behaviors. By slightly altering the objective to research the potential correlation between leadership styles (behaviors are outward expressions of leadership style) and performance, the obstacle vanished. Research builds on what has come before, to take advantage of the prior scholarly work of experts. Doctoral research requires using existing knowledge, including existing and established data collection instruments.

Validity

The validity of the study establishes the integrity of a researcher's findings and conclusions (Oleinik, 2011). Qualitative researchers strive for strong internal validity, which refers to the justification and confirmation of stated conclusions about causal relationships between variables (Bleijenbergh, Korzilius, & Verschuren, 2011; Stone-Romero & Rosopa, 2010). As a quantitative researcher, Jones (2013) strove for a high degree of external validity. External validity refers to the generalization of the results from a sample population to the total population, and the ability of another researcher to conduct the same study in a different setting and arrive at similar if not the same conclusion (Wahyuni, 2012). Because of meticulously documenting the data collection, coding, and analysis procedures, and using a reliable survey, the Jones study contained strong external validity, a necessary component of a quantitative study (Oleinik, 2011).

Sample Size

Qualitative researchers have the advantage regarding sample size. Creswell (2009) denoted that 15 – 20 participants are a sufficient sample size to conduct qualitative research. Quantitative researchers must use a sample size calculator to determine the minimum sample size required to produce statistically significant results. In Jones' (2013) study, the initial sample size was 26, computed with a simple, sample size calculator retrieved from the Internet. A doctoral reviewer challenged the minimum sample size, expertly denoting that in quantitative research the requirement of a larger sample size to produce statistically significant results. With the target population, geographic region, and data collection procedures based on a sample size of 26, Jones faced a major obstacle, yet refractive thinking facilitated finding the solution. Through encouragement and a *conquering the problem* spirit, sound advice prompted searching for an appropriate expert. In the spirit of cooperation and further discovery, Jones contacted a local university statistician with expert knowledge of calculating a proper sample size through justifiable means. Following the statistician's advice resulted in using G*Power 3.1.5 sample size calculator, developed by Faul, Erdlelder, Buchner, and Lang (2009). The G*Power 3.1.5 calculator is simple, yet statistically sophisticated in that the sample size is specific to the planned testing procedures (Faul et al., 2009). By obtaining expert advice, calculating the appropriate sample size of 67 for the proposed statistical testing procedures became unproblematic. Jones avoided doctoral *paralysis*, solved the problem satisfactorily to all committee members, resulting in approval of the proposal.

The challenge of the doctoral quest lies in how to look at the options available to decide the most appropriate path to travel. Remember, doctoral scholars do not need to know all the answers; they merely need to know how to find the answers or those who can help in search of solving the problem. The pursuit of a doctorate might be a difficult quest, yet should not be a lonely journey. Although friends and family members do provide encouragement, inspiration, and support, building relationships with experts provides the means to travel around, over, and through the obstacles.

Ethics, Data Collection, Analysis, and Findings

Researchers have an obligation to examine the ethical considerations of a proposed study (White & Fitzgerald, 2010). An ethical student-researcher protects participants, the educational institution, and the researcher from ethical violations (White & Fitzgerald, 2010). A researcher must guard against harming participants, which includes emotional, mental, physical, or professional injury (Sikes & Piper, 2010). In the Jones (2013) study, the target population received: (a) an invitation to participate that outlined the purpose of the study and provided assurances of confidentiality; (b) an informed consent form disclosing the purpose of the research, sample survey questions, the participants' rights to privacy and right to refuse participation, and contact information for the educational institution and the researcher; and (c) the MLQ survey. Individually assigned numeric codes negated the need for participants to enter their names or signatures. The informed consent form clearly delineated the voluntary nature of the study and the opportunity to withdraw from the study at any time. Voluntary participation is an essential element of ethical research (Sikes & Piper, 2010).

Mind Garden, Inc., the licensor of the MLQ survey, offered Jones (2013) several options: (a) an anonymous Internet survey; (b) an Internet survey that provides participant identifiers; and (c) a licensing arrangement to allow printing copies and mailing the survey. The intent of the Jones study required identifying the leadership style of each participant to couple the style with the participant's organizational financial performance; therefore, the Internet survey that did not provide participant-specific data was not an option. The remaining Internet-based option required participants to enter a username and create a password prior to completing the survey. Although a lack confidence level of attaining the minimum sample size existed, Jones initially selected the Internet option because of the speed, price, and ease of e-mailing the survey. Questions abounded regarding the effectiveness of the Internet MLQ survey. Would busy, organizational leaders take the time to complete the survey? Would the survey land in spam folders across the southern United States? What effect would the requirement to enter a user name and password prior to actually viewing the survey have on the response rate? Many self-reflecting questions begged to be asked, yet few problem-solving answers existed to overcome the Jones' dilemma regarding the survey method.

Doctoral research is much like many life experiences; when one is not at ease, holding doubts or uneasy intuitions, engaging in further investigation and critical thinking is a wise strategy. Jones' (2013) doctoral chair provided numerous warnings regarding response rates from top executives. Busy professionals require more than an e-mail from a doctoral student to respond, even from a colleague they may know. For Jones to proceed, two pathways existed: locating fact-based information and assurances of the success rate of the Internet survey or a change of course. The solution to the dilemma arrived during the oral defense of the proposal. The second committee member questioned the data collection method, revealing expert knowledge of conducting surveys. Never one to shy away from expert advice, Jones knew the opportunity to overcome the obstacle was at hand. The committee member shared personal and professional experiences of 3-5%

response rates to Internet surveys and 20-30% response rates to mailed surveys. Jones changed direction, mailed the survey along with a personalized invitation to participate to the 348 target general managers, and attained the minimum sample size of 67 eight days after mailing. Doctoral success was one chapter away.

Using Predictive Analytics Software, Jones (2013) analyzed the numerically coded data, revealing a significant relationship between leadership style and financial performance. Additionally, the findings indicated a positive relationship between transactional leadership style and performance, and a negative relationship between laissez-faire leadership style and performance. Why are these correlational findings relevant and important to rural electric cooperatives as well as other organizational leaders? The positive relationship between transactional leaders and performance indicates that when leaders employ transactional behaviors, such as staying involved in the operational aspects of the company, performance tends to be strong. The negative relationship between laissez-faire leaders and performance indicates that when general managers avoid leadership duties, financial performance suffers. When leaders exhibit few, if any, laissez-faire behaviors, performance thrives. Leadership style relates to financial performance; the manner in which a leader behaves, communicates, and operates affects employees, profitability, and organizational performance (De Vries, Bakker-Pieper, & Oostenveld, 2010; Jones, 2013).

Conclusion

Conducting research involving professional colleagues might evoke numerous obstacles for doctoral students, yet studying a problem within an affiliated organization or industry provides personal and professional rewards. The quantitative method provides an excellent means to accomplish the objective without jeopardizing the study's integrity, reliability, or validity. By mitigating the potential for inclusion of researcher bias, the quantitative method provides researchers the opportunity to conduct a study of academic and professional worth, ultimately satisfying the initial catalyst of curiosity.

Completing the capstone study of a doctoral degree is a demanding process, with plenty of obstacles. Maintaining a philosophy of *never giving up* regardless of the challenges, required revisions, or academic criticisms is essential. Upon reflection of the doctoral process, Jones readily admits many self-induced problems and obstacles. Academic advisors suggested the use of writing and grammar technology tools, yet just completing a Master's degree produced a misguided attitude of superiority regarding scholarly writing and formatting style. Wasting weeks rewriting sections of the study provided a memorable learning experience. Avoid stumbling into the minimum sample size calculation. Jones explored the process after creating a problem. Conducting the investigation, gaining the knowledge, or at a minimum, contacting an expert with knowledge of sample size calculations prior to faltering is a wiser strategy and a lesson learned. When anxiety, intuition, or suspicion enters, proceed with caution. Refractive thinkers might make every attempt to overcome an obstacle, yet a primary objective is to succeed through perseverance, not fail because of stubbornness, flawed opinions, or unfounded confidence. Jones' most significant learned lesson is doctoral advisors, committee members, and academic and professional experts are the most important resource available to complete a terminal degree. The process of doctoral scholarship at its core includes the ability to learn how to accept, solicit, and treasure constructive critique. Do not waste the opportunity to learn from experts. Build relationships early, respect experience and expertise, call on mentors often, and avoid creating obstacles through a mistaken mindset of *I already know everything.*

Doctoral researchers should recognize that completing a study is a team effort. Although the formal team consists of university committee members and academic advisors, doctoral students can access the expert knowledge of refractive thinkers to move beyond the obstacles. As denoted by Dr. Lentz, refractive thinkers do not just think *outside the box*, they redefine the box, and never relinquish the pursuit of knowledge because of problems, frustrations, or barriers.

References

Amitabh, M., & Gupta, R. K. (2010). Research in strategy-structure-performance construct: Review of trends, paradigms and methodologies. *Journal of Management and Organization, 16*, 744-763. doi:10.5172/jmo.2010.16.5.744

Bass, B., & Avolio, B. (2004). *Multifactor leadership questionnaire: Manual and sample set* (3rd ed.). Redwood City, CA: Mind Garden.

Bleijenbergh, I., Korzilius, H., & Verschuren, P. (2011). Methodological criteria for the internal validity and utility of practice oriented research. *Quality and Quantity, 45*(1), 145-156. doi:10.1007/s11135-010-9361-5

Brahma, S. S. (2009). Assessment of construct validity in management research: A structured guideline. *Journal of Management Research, 9*, 59-71. Retrieved from http://www.indianjournals.com/ijor.aspz?target=ijor:jmr&type=home

Creswell, J. W. (2009). *Research design: Qualitative, quantitative, and mixed methods approaches* (3rd ed.). Thousand Oaks, CA: Sage.

De Vries, R. E., Bakker-Pieper, A., & Oostenveld, W. (2010). Leadership = communication? The relations of leaders' communication styles with leadership styles, knowledge sharing and leadership outcomes. *Journal of Business & Psychology, 25*, 367-380. doi:10.1007/s10869-009-9140-2

Faul, F., Erdlelder, E., Buchner, A., & Lang, A. (2009). Statistical power analyses using G*Power 3.1: Tests for correlation and regression analyses. *Behavior Research Methods, 41*, 1149-1160. doi:10.3758/BRM.41.4.1149

Fielding, N. (2010). Mixed methods research in the real world. *International Journal of Social Research Methodology, 13*, 127-138. doi:10.1080/13645570902996186

Jones, R. C. (2013). *Examining leadership styles and financial performance within rural electric cooperatives.* Manuscript submitted for publication.

Labaree, D. F. (2011). The lure of statistics for educational researchers. *Educational Theory, 61*, 621-632. doi:10.1111/j.1741-5446.2011.00424.x

Leong, L. C., & Fischer, R. (2011). Is transformational leadership universal? A meta-analytical investigation of multifactor leadership questionnaire means across cultures. *Journal of Leadership & Organizational Studies 18*(2), 164-174. doi:10.1177/1548051810385003

National rural electric cooperative association [NRECA]. (2012). *Homepage.* Retrieved from http//:www.nreca.org/

Oleinik, A. (2011). Mixing quantitative and qualitative content analysis: Triangulation at work. *Quality and Quantity, 45,* 859-873. doi:10.1007/s11135-010-9399-4

Parab, S., & Bhalerao, S. (2010). Study designs. *International Journal of Ayurveda Research, 1,* 128-131. doi:10.4103/0974-7788.64406

Sadeghi, A., & Pihie, Z. (2012). Transformational leadership and its predictive effects on leadership effectiveness. *International Journal of Business & Social Science, 3*(7), 186-197. Retrieved from http://www.ijbssnet.com

Sikes, P., & Piper, H. (2010). Ethical research, academic freedom and the role of ethics committees and review procedures in educational research. *International Journal of Research & Method in Education, 33,* 205-213. doi:10.1080/1743727X.2010.511838

Stone-Romero, E., & Rosopa, P. J. (2010). Research design options for testing mediation models and their implications for facets of validity. *Journal of Managerial Psychology, 25,* 697-712. doi:10.1108/02683941011075256

Symonds, J. E., & Gorard, S. (2010). Death of mixed methods? Or the rebirth of research as a craft. *Evaluation & Research in Education, 23,* 121-136. doi:10.1080/09500790.2010.483514

Wahyuni, D. (2012). The research design maze: Understanding paradigms, cases, methods and methodologies. *Journal of Applied Management Accounting Research, 10*(1), 69-80. Retrieved from http://www.cmawebline.org/jamar

White, J., & Fitzgerald, T. (2010). Researcher tales and research ethics: the spaces in which we find ourselves. *International Journal of Research & Method in Education, 33,* 273-285. doi:10.1080/174372 7X.2010.511711

About the Author...

Dr. Ronald C. Jones resides in the historic town of DeFuniak Springs, Florida. Dr. Ron holds several accredited degrees; a Bachelor of Science (BS) in Management from the University of West Florida; a Master of Business Administration (MBA) from Liberty University; and a Doctorate of Business Administration (DBA) from Walden University.

Dr. Ron is an Associate Faculty Member at Ashford University, approved to teach business, management, and real estate courses. He enjoys the interaction with students, striving to provide a pathway to academic excellence within the classroom. He is a member of the Southern Management Association and Sigma Beta Delta Business Honor Society.

Dr. Ron is President and CEO of Ronald C. Jones, Inc., a land development company. He holds professional licenses in real estate and contracting. He also serves on two corporate boards; President and Chairman of the Board of Choctawhatchee Electric Cooperative, Inc. and board member of PowerSouth Energy Cooperative, Inc. His doctoral study, *Examining Leadership Styles and Financial Performance within Rural Electric Cooperatives,* provided him the opportunity to gain professional and academic expertise to facilitate improvements in the rural electric industry.

To reach Dr. Ronald C. Jones for information on consulting or doctoral coaching, please e-mail: rcjones@earthlink.net

About the Author...

Southern Nevadan author Dr. Cheryl A. Lentz holds several accredited degrees; a Bachelor of Arts (BA) from the University of Illinois, Urbana-Champaign; a Master of Science in International Relations (MSIR) from Troy University; and a Doctorate of Management (DM) in Organizational Leadership from the University of Phoenix School of Advanced Studies. She has her Sloan C Certification from Colorado State University–Global, as well as her Quality Matters Peer Reviewer (APP/PRC) Certification.

Dr. Cheryl, affectionately known as 'Doc C' to her students, is a university professor on faculty with Colorado State University-Global, Embry-Riddle University, University of Phoenix, The University of the Rockies, and Walden University. Dr. Cheryl serves as a dissertation committee member, faculty mentor, is a dissertation coach, and also offers expertise in editing for APA style for graduate thesis and doctoral dissertations.

Dr. Cheryl is also an active member of Alpha Sigma Alpha Sorority.

She is a prolific author known for her writings on *The Golden Palace Theory of Management* and refractive thinking. Additional published works include her dissertation: *Strategic Decision Making in Organizational Performance: A Quantitative Study of Employee Inclusiveness, The Golden Palace Theory of Management, Journey Outside the Golden Palace, The Consumer Learner: Emerging Expectations of a Customer Service Mentality*, and contributions to award winning series: *The Refractive Thinker*® *: Anthology of Doctoral Learners* , Volumes I-VII.

To reach Dr. Cheryl Lentz for information on refractive thinking, doctoral coaching, or any of these topics, please visit her website: http://drcheryllentz.com or e-mail: drcheryllentz@gmail.com

CHAPTER 4
To Better Understand a Case Study

By Dr. Bryan T. Shaw & Dr. Xavier Bruce

Conducting research can seem overwhelming during the brainstorming process. First, the need to conduct research has to be identified. The researcher then spends time brainstorming about how to best approach the research topic and obtain the necessary the data. Neuman (2003) noted the goal of research is to identify common themes that generalize to similar situations. Once the researcher determines the research goal, the researcher must choose the most appropriate design in conducting the study. The design of the study organizes the research and helps design a course of action to complete the research. There are many designs available for the researcher to choose from to conduct the investigation. Sufficient time should be dedicated to plan a study to avoid any mishaps (Yin, 2009).

The nature of the study leads a researcher to choose one particular design over another. However, based on experience and knowledge, the researcher selects the most appropriate research design. The research design could be used to keep the research process on topic or make slight modifications to the study as needed. Researchers enjoy the flexibility of changing focus and developing new research questions in a case study design.

This chapter provides clarity on the use of a case study design. To offer an understanding about case study, the researchers explain what a case study design is and how the case study could be used in application. Also, this chapter will indicate how sampling is affected by theory-building using a case study design. Several books and articles include similar components of a case study; therefore this chapter is focused toward providing a clear and to-the point overview. The proceeding information could be helpful to researcher seeking a different perspective for using a case study design.

Defining Case Study

A well-planned research design, in the beginning of any type of research, helps the researcher navigate through the process and improve the odds of a quality study. Yin (2009) noted that a design is the plan that guides the research process. This plan allows the researcher to organize the study and minimize confusion. Keep in mind, conducting a study can be time-consuming and costly depending on the scope of the study. Therefore, developing a well-developed plan at the onset of the study could prove beneficial to the researcher. With the proper design, a researcher can keep the research focused on the topic areas and developing pertinent research questions in which applicable to obtain the relevant data. Yin further noted that case studies consist of five critical components to include: study questions, propositions if any, units of analysis, logical linking of data, and criteria for interpreting data.

Depending on the scope of the study, conducting research can be a daunting task. Once the researcher decides to research a particular topic, the researcher selects a design. Sounds simple, but research design selection is paramount in a rigorous study. Selecting a design is just as important as the research topic. During the time of conducting his research, Shaw (2012) did not initially choose a case study design. He dedicated a considerable amount of time to learning about case studies that ultimately lead to the selection of a case study design. Shaw devoted multiple hours to researching the various research designs in attempts to select the most appropriate design to guide the research and collect the needed data. After considering the problem statement, research question, and acquiring the needed data, Shaw elected to use the case study design. Consequently, this chapter is geared toward experiences gained using a case study design. A few definitions may benefit researchers contemplating the case study design: a) Case studies are descriptive, which allows the researcher to observe an individual or organization in a unique setting (Salkind, 2003, p. 212); b) Merriam Webster's collegiate dictionary (1995, p. 177) defined a case study as an intensive analysis of an individual unit (as a person or community) stressing developmental factors in relation to environment; and c) an intensive study of one unit with the goal to generalize across a larger set of units (Gerring, 2004, p. 341).

The researcher could apply a case study design to investigate one phenomenon in a particular setting. Therefore, if a researcher explores a single phenomenon, the case study design could be helpful. If the researcher selects the case study design, how could the design be applied to a particular study?

Application

Case study design allows the researcher to observe a social phenomenon and apply it to either qualitative or quantitative methods (Terrell, 2009). This type of flexibility allows the researcher the option to investigate a phenomenon regardless of the method. Flexibility gives the researcher the necessary latitude to make modifications where needed to enhance the study. Shaw

(2012) chose to use a case study design in his study to investigate enterprise resource planning systems in a local government organization using the qualitative method. With a qualitative approach, the researcher collects data through the views of participants (Creswell, 2009). As such, based on the dichotomy of the methodology the case study could have been applied using the quantitative method as well.

Case studies are also very useful in a learning environment. Institutions of higher learning use case studies as an education medium (Soukup, 2003). Prior to realizing benefits, students learn via a case study design. The use of case studies, if done thoroughly, could be just as effective as statistical analysis (Achen & Snidal, 1989). The case study is used to view a particular phenomenon in detail. The benefit to using a case study design is that it offers an in-depth analysis of the investigation, and obtains data or viewpoints from a specific entity. A limitation of the case study design would be only capturing the experiences and the viewpoints from only one entity.

A case study is limited to just one phenomenon, but a benefit from using a case study design is that multiple case studies could be investigated for synthesis (Houghton, Casey, Shaw, & Murphy, 2013). Comparing and contrasting the data obtained from multiple cases could prove beneficial to the researcher. As mentioned, Shaw (2012) used a single-case study design to investigate ERP systems in local government. The study focused on just one organization. What if the single case study was expanded to investigate 4 individual local governments? Each local government would be investigated separately in full detail. From a researcher's perspective, on may achieve knowledge through each investigation. Also, the researcher could view case studies collectively; realizing the benefits from single case study analyses or multiple case study analyses.

Case studies may also provide a deeper understanding of the phenomena discovered in quantitative studies. Bruce (2011) used a quantitative cross-sectional survey study to investigate the impact of professional and personal characteristics on the use of influence strategies. Bruce discovered statistically significance between (a) ethnicity and use of rationality and (b) education and use of rationality. Although some authors criticize case studies for offering less value, lower generalizability, and greater researcher bias, a case study is the next logical step to explore the two aforementioned relationships (Runeson & Host, 2009). What the case study lacks in experimental control, this design makes up for in offering multiple sources of evidence and richness (Runeson & Host, 2009). Case studies often use quantitative data; however, this research method fails to control the context of the study (Gibbert & Ruigrok, 2010).

The Bruce (2012) study revealed numeric data, which described the attitude of a sample population. In future research, a case study may yield explanatory context to the findings. Runeson and Host (2009) suggested that the increased control that quantitative studies offer may reduce the degree of realism and set influential factors outside the scope of the study. Although case studies involve a relatively lower level of control, they imply a realism that provides deeper and richer explanations than quantitative studies. Even though case studies may be less precise than quantitative studies, their broadness and flexibility aid in explaining dynamic, real world phenomena (Runeson & Host, 2009).

When the target audience's primary interest include subjects such as advanced technology, mathematical analysis, engineering mechanics, and logistics, the audience is likely to value quantitative data more than qualitative data from case studies (Bruce, 2011). One reason these audience may prefer quantitative studies over case studies is rigor. Often seen as a weakness of case studies, rigor in quantitative research is subject to standardized procedures and codified methods of assessment (Gibbert & Ruigrok, 2010). Whereas a quantitative study may reveal statistical significance, a case study allows the researcher to 'peel back the onion' to investigate influential factors.

Expanding Research

Bruce (2011) did not use a case study design to guide his research and chose to collect quantitative survey data to produce statistically based results pertinent to the study. Understanding that each research design has limitations, he was able share how a case study design may inform further his research and add additional value. Houghton et al., (2013) asserted how rigorous researcher can be attained using a qualitative case study. The authors further explained how rigor can be attained through credibility, dependability, confirmability, and transferability. Research is a dynamic tool in gathering information and expanding on earlier research. Each research design has a specific purpose depending on the needs of the researcher. A case study design is just one on many design used to achieve research results.

A case study design could be used explore a phenomenon initially, and then same phenomenon can be tested, or further expanded upon using different research design. As mentioned earlier, Shaw (2012) did not initially choose to use a case study design to explore the factors of an ERP system. The Delphi method, grounded theory, phenomenological, and ethnographic were considered for the study but were not chosen. The Delphi method was the first choice based on initial research a conversation with a colleague. However, based on subsequent research concerning the Delphi, the case study design was ultimately selected. The Delphi works on the premise of an expert perspective regarding the future state of a phenomenon (Terrell, 2009). The Delphi method would have been used if the researcher wanted to gather the insight from an expert panel on a *future* viewpoint of a particular phenomenon (Hanafizadeh & Mirzazadeh, 2011).

Investigating a particular phenomenon involves a significant amount of research. The researcher is responsible for determining the scope of the research and the overall process; thus multiple scenarios may be considered during the research process. Therefore, research design selection is paramount to help conduct a valid and reliable study (Rose & Cray, 2013). The research design is a plan to explore, test, or expand research. Expanding on previous research adds value through different viewpoints and research designs. Thus, a case study design can be use as an initial study or expand the knowledge of an earlier study.

Sampling Using Case Study Design

Once the researcher decides to investigate a phenomenon in its natural setting using qualitative or quantitative methods, a case study design could be applied. Case studies can be used either in a qualitative or quantitative method, which allows the researcher flexibility. Case studies are descriptive, which affords the researcher the opportunity to observe an individual or organization in a unique or natural setting (Salkind, 2003). Observing a phenomenon in a natural setting is an ideal way to collect the relevant data. In doing so, the researcher is not trying to re-create an environment in which to conduct the study. Case studies are intended to understand the how and why the phenomenon is behaving in a particular manner, and the natural setting would produce the more representative data.

The use of a case study helps the researcher to determine the sample, as the researcher is focused on one phenomenon to investigate. Sample sizes of a qualitative study using a case study design tend to vary in size, but are usually small (Cooper &

Schindler, 2006). The empirical data could then be collected from the participants via surveys or interview questions. Considering Shaw (2012) used a case study design, the author chose to interview the participants in their natural setting since he had direct access to them. So, using the right design at the onset of the study allowed Shaw to stay on topic and keep the study focused on the research question. Once the data have been collected, the researcher could arrange the data mining software package for analyses.

The purpose of research is to acquire a better understanding of a phenomenon. According to Garge (2009, p. 59) "all social researchers, whether using qualitative or quantitative methods, are driven by the search for understanding, operate from epistemological bases, and address methodological concerns about reliability, validity, and the ability to generalize." Therefore, using a case study design seeks to understand how a phenomenon is behaving in a natural setting. As such, data collected using qualitative research with a case study design gives the researcher valuable information to understand the phenomenon better (Neuman, 2003).

Based on the design, purposeful sampling should be incorporated when using a case study. Purpose sampling occurs when the researcher deliberately chooses participants because of unique characteristics concerning the subject matter (Cooper & Schindler, 2006). Using a case study, once the phenomenon to investigate has been determined, then, by default, the researcher is also selecting the population to sample. Seawright and Gerring (2008) argued against random sampling using a case study design. Basically, when using a case study, the researcher decides to study a particular phenomenon. Therefore, the need to select a random sample in no longer needed, which represents an example where the research design dictates the population to sample.

Sampling or scaled down models enables the researcher to make inferences about the larger society (Neuman, 2003). The case study design has already focused the study to investigate a phenomenon, allowing for a more focused population. Therefore, the collected data is derived from a specific group of participants with unique characteristics. A case study design steers the researcher into a purposeful sample. Walshe (2011) suggested that case studies are designed to investigate a bound phenomenon. The sample is bound by the phenomenon being investigated.

Theory Building

After the researcher collects the relevant data for study, various analyses can be performed. With the methodology selected, the case study design has afforded the researcher the plan for conducting the research. In the event the qualitative methodology was chosen, the research can be expanded beyond analytical analysis. Qualitative researchers tend to use this method for generating theories during from the collected data. Case study design can be helpful to develop theories. Neuman (2003) argued that many researchers use the grounded theory due to flexibility. Although Gibbert and Ruigrok (2010) discovered that the academic community perceives case studies that build theory as most interesting and impactful, a case study alone is insufficient for generating theories (Diaz, 2009). Ideally, a case study results supports a generalizable theory applicable to similar phenomenon.

A case study is a useful tool in many ways, but in the pursuit of theory building, needs other research design support; therefore, in Shaw (2012) a theory was not generated. Instead, the purpose of the study was to explore why a phenomenon was occurring in a particular setting. The study available for future students to build upon the study and pursue theory building if so desired. Therefore, case study design coupled with the grounded theory could be powerful tool for the researcher. Yin (1994) noted five pertinent areas of a research design important for case studies: a.) the research questions; b.) its propositions; c.) units of analysis; d.) critical and logical thinking; and e.) criteria for interpreting the findings. Each of the five primary areas focus mentioned can prove valuable to a researcher regardless of methodology or research design. View the five primary areas of research as critical elements that will assist the researcher in conducting an objective and rigorous study. (Yin, 1994)

Conclusion

Conducting research can be achieved through numerous designs. This chapter was focused on case study research. With an increased understanding of the case study design, a researcher may introduce more rigor to a study. This chapter opened with an introduction on how research is influenced using a case study design. This chapter provided an overview on how to use of a case study design. To offer an understanding about case study, this chapter focused on a case study design uses, base on the literature and how the case study could be used in application or research. Shaw and Bruce discussed how a case study design could add value in future research and their previous works. Sampling, theory building, and expanding research, and were also covered in this chapter. Several books and articles have been written discussing a case study design; therefore, the goal of this chapter was to provide a clear and to-the point overview on elements of a case study design. The information contained in this chapter could be helpful to researchers looking for a different perspective about case study research.

References

Achen, C., & Snidal, D. (1989). Rational deterrence theory and comparative case studies. *World Politics, 41*(2), 143-169. Retrieved from http://www.jstor.org/stable/2010405

Bruce, X. V. (2011). *The impact of demographic and professional characteristics on group purchasing organizations' use of rational persuasion* (Doctoral dissertation). Retrieved from ProQuest Dissertations and Theses Database. (UMI No. 3482188)

Cooper, D., & Schindler, P. (2006). *Business research methods* (9th ed.). New York, NY: McGraw-Hill Irwin.

Creswell, J. W. (2009). *Research design: Qualitative, quantitative, and mixed methods approaches* (3rd ed.). Thousand Oaks, CA: Sage.

Díaz Adrade, A. (2009). Interpretive research aiming at theory building: Adopting and adapting the case study design. *The Qualitative Report, 14*(1), 42-60. Retrieved from http://www.nova.edu/ssss/QR/QR14-1/diaz-andrade.pdf

Gerring, J. (2004). What is a case study and what is it good for? *The American Political Science Review, 98*, 341-354.

Gibbert, M., & Ruigrok, W. (2010). The "what" and "how" of case study rigor: Three strategies based on published research. *Organizational Research Methods, 13*, 710-737. doi:10.1177/1094428109351319

Hanafizadeh, P., & Mirzazadeh, M. (2011). Visualizing market segmentation using self-organizing maps and Fuzzy Delphi method–ADSL market of a telecommunication company. *Expert Systems with Applications, 38*, 198-205. doi:10.1016/j.eswa.2010.06.045

Houghton, C., Casey, D., Shaw, D., & Murphy, K. (2013). Rigour in qualitative case-study research. *Nurse Researcher, 20*(4), 12-17. Retrieved from http://www.ncbi.nlm.nih.gov/pubmed/23520707

Lori, S. S. (2003). Applied management and decision sciences/finance case study. *Futurics, 27*(3), 26-46. Retrieved from http://www.homeworkmarket.com/sites/default/files/applied_management_and_decisions_-_soukup.pdf

Neuman, W. (2003). *Social research methods: Qualitative and quantitative approaches* (5th ed.). Boston, MA: Pearson Education.

Rose, W. R., & Cray, D. (2013). Validating and enhancing a strategy transformation model using case study. *Global Business & Management Research, 5*(1), 32-53.

Runeson, P., & Host, M. (2009). Guidelines for conducting and reporting case study research in software engineering. *Emprical Software Engineering, 14,* 131-164. doi:10.1007/s10664-008-9102-8

Salkind, N. (2003). *Exploring research* (5th ed.). Upper Saddle River, NJ: Prentice Hall.

Shaw, B. (2012). *Exploring the factors of an ERP System in a Local Government Organization* (Unpublished doctoral dissertation). Retrieved from ProQuest Dissertations and Theses Database. (UMI No. 3510463)

Terrell, R. (2009). Determining an effective and future enterprise architecture in the federal government: A Delphi study (Doctoral dissertation). Retrieved from ProQuest Dissertation and Theses database. (UMI No. 3355061)

Walshe, C. (2011). The evaluation of complex interventions in palliative care: An exploration of the potential of case study research strategies. *Palliative Medicine, 25,* 774-81. doi:10.1177/0269216311419883

Yin, R. (1994). Case study research: Design and methods. Beverly Hills, CA: Sage.

Yin, R. (2009). *Case study research: Design and methods.* Thousand Oaks, CA: Sage.

About the Author...

Dr. Bryan T. Shaw holds several accredited degrees; a Bachelor of Science (BS) from Upper Iowa University; a Master of Business Administration (MBA) from University of Phoenix, and a Doctorate of Business Administration (DBA) in Information Systems Management from Walden University.

Dr. Bryan is also known as 'Dr. B' to his students. Dr. Bryan is an adjunct faculty member with University of Phoenix (Savannah, GA Campus) and Columbia College (Ft. Stewart, GA Campus).

Dr. Bryan served honorably in the U.S. Army for 5 years. He is currently a Services Management Administrator for a local government organization where he is primarily responsible for managing the operating and capital budgets.

Dr. Bryan plans and develops yearly goals and objectives for the department. He is focused on strategic planning and analytical decision-making. With a strong background in budget management and operational procedures, Dr. Bryan positions the department for optimal efficiencies.

Dr. Bryan is an author known for his writing on *Enterprise Resource Planning (ERP) Systems in a Local Government.*

To reach Dr. Bryan T. Shaw for additional information, please email: drshawbt@gmail.com

About the Author...

Dr. Xavier V. Bruce holds several accredited degrees; a Bachelor of Science (BS) in Biology from the United States Air Force Academy; Master of Business Administration in Information Systems Management from Wayland Baptist University; and a Doctorate of Business Administration (DBA) in Global Supply Chain Management from Walden University. He has his Professional Coaching Certification from the Institute of Professional Excellence in Coaching (iPEC) and is a Diplomat and Credentialed Fellow in the American Academy of Medical Administrators (CFAAMA). He is an Energy Leadership Master Practitioner (ELI-MP) and Certified Lean Six Sigma Green Belt (CLSSGB).

Dr. Xavier, affectionately known as 'Professor X' is an adjunct instructor on faculty with Colorado Technical University. He is also Walden University Alumni Ambassador. Dr. Xavier serves as an academic and life coach offering expertise to students in overcoming inner and outer blocks to successfully completing their thesis or dissertation.

He is an author known for his writings on *The Impact of Demographic and Professional Characteristics on Group Purchasing Organizations' Use of Rational Persuasion and Influence Strategies in Health Care GPOs* and strategic influence theory.

To reach Dr. Xavier Bruce for information on strategic influence theory, thesis and dissertation coaching, or Energy Leadership, please visit his website: www.up2lift.com or email: xavier.bruce@up2lift.com

CHAPTER 5

Comparative Study on Mortgage Lending Practices to
Minority Borrowers
in the Atlanta, Georgia Area

by Dr. Coleen Melissa James

To own a home a dream of most Americans. However, for many minorities, owning a home brings many challenges because of the lack of awareness amid an influx of predatory lending practices. Predatory lending is as when lenders invoke excessive and unnecessary fees, or coerce borrowers into high-interest rate loans (over 10%), when they could qualify for better prime rates (Bailey, 2005). The research question is a relevant topic because the goal of the James (2013) study was to uncover factors behind minorities victimized by predatory lending practices.

The purpose of The Georgia Fair Lending Act (GAFLA) is to help the elderly, people with sub-prime credit, and individuals not sophisticated about handling money. However with GAFLA in place since 2002, if an investor purchases a mortgage-backed security that includes a loan covered by the GAFLA law, he or she is not responsible if the originating lender practiced predatory lending. The purpose of the law is to protect borrowers from prepayment penalties, balloon payments, and other fees on high-interest loans.

Overview of Study

The American Dream of owning a home has many challenges for minority homeowners because some lack awareness and opportunities to use traditional lenders. The James' (2013) study is of critical importance to U.S. society because many minorities are still not aware of the many lending options available to them, both within and beyond their neighborhoods in the Atlanta Metropolitan area. Homeownership brings a sense of pride to individuals and their communities. There are also tax benefits for homeownership that one cannot receive as a renter (Bailey, 2005).

The goal of the James (2013) study was to identify disparities between the four races (African American, Asian Americans, White Americans, and Hispanic Americans) as in relation to lending practices in the Metro Atlanta area, both before and after the real estate bubble of 2007. These communities need housing advocates and educators to focus not only on increasing rates of homeownership, but also on helping families avoid late payments and foreclosures. Knowledgeable assistance often helps prevent families from falling into the disturbing position of getting assets they cannot afford (Tyuse & Birkenmaier, 2006).

James (2013) conducted a qualitative study on mortgage lending practices to minority borrowers in the Atlanta, Georgia, area. The study compared the treatment of African-Americans, Asian-Americans, and Hispanic-Americans vs. their White-American counterparts in relation to obtaining a mortgage loan. The author interviewed real estate professionals in the Atlanta Metro area of varying races. More specifically, the researcher interviewed African-American, Asian-American, Hispanic-American, and White-American real estate agents. The hope of the study was to uncover gaps that persist in the mortgage industry between minorities and White Americans. In many cases, the real estate agent is the start to the homeownership process.

Background

Owning a home is probably the most expensive asset in a person's financial portfolio. Real Estate is an asset that can survive individuals as an inheritance to children and grandchildren, if properly managed. Shapiro (2004) further stated that the transfer of wealth for college assistance, down payment assistance for a first home, and inheritances may give recipients an advantage in life. Shapiro stated that when persons are recipients of an inheritance, they have a sense of entitlement and experience a disconnection with persons and races less fortunate.

According to results from a study conducted by the Pew Charitable Trust (2008), 1 in 33 homeowners in the United States will experience a foreclosure in their lifetime because of subprime loans. According to the study, 1 in 27 homeowners defaulted on the home loan because of a subprime loan in the state of Georgia. Because of the numerous foreclosures, many homeowners not in foreclosure will have their property value decline because of the numerous foreclosures in the community (Pew Charitable Trust, 2008). Based upon this study, Georgia was in the top 10 of states most affected by foreclosure, listed at number seven in the United States, and foreclosures affects persons with prime loans and a strong credit history.

Bailey (2005) stated that the Center for Responsible Lending found that borrowers in predominantly African-American neighborhoods are more likely than other races to receive loans with a prepayment penalty, which are expensive fees charged for paying the loan off early. The study conducted by the Center for Responsible Lending (2005) took into consideration factors, such as creditworthiness, which could affect whether a lender invokes a penalty. The purpose of the James (2013) study was to identify if preferences given to borrowers based on race or ethnicity in the Atlanta area before the real estate bubble burst and afterwards existed.

Champagne (2012) recounts the U.S. Senate Committee (2012) noted that legislators realize that predatory lending does not only affect minorities and their communities, but also surrounding communities. Many of the predatory practices by large banks such as Citi, Countrywide, and Wells Fargo are the catalyst of the U.S. national housing collapse. Assistant Attorney General Perez noted that African-American and Hispanic-American communities experienced a great financial setback by the housing collapse. The committee noted numerous accounts of African Americans and Hispanic Americans who stated that they could have obtained prime loans, but professionals steered them into high interest subprime loans, with a higher risk of defaulting on the loan.

The housing crisis created changes in the financial conditions of many minority families and communities across the United States. The average home value has reduced since 2005. The reduction in value has stripped many families of the equity they had in their homes. Maintaining the high mortgage payments became a challenge. In many cases, the homes were worth less than the mortgaged amount. Because of the decline in home values, 1 in 33 homeowners faced foreclosure (RealtyTrac, 2009).

Foreclosures disproportionately affect minority homes and neighborhoods. Kalil and Wightman (2009) stated that middle-class minorities are more prone to suffer from the after-effects of a job loss. Depreciating home values and high foreclosure rates have a similar effect on middle class minorities. This occurrence exacerbates the existing racial inequalities and broadens the achievement gap.

Georgia Department of Community Affairs (2008) recounts in 2007, the state of Georgia ranked seventh in the United States for households facing foreclosure. Georgia also ranked ninth in the country for loans made by subprime lenders. Georgia ranked eighth in the percentage of owner-occupied loan purchases made to low income borrowers. In the first quarter of 2008, Georgia was among 10 states with seriously delinquent mortgages. In the Southeast region, Georgia had a rate of 1.3 per thousand households classified as real estate owned (REO) (Georgia Department of Community Affairs, 2008).

The low-income community needs these financial institutions to rise to the occasion. Seidman and Tescher (2005) stated these financial institutions needs new strategies and implement new product design as well as enhance their marketing and their outreach approach. These financial institutions need to be more customers service-oriented, and more upper management support is needed. These institutions must do more than persuade low-income customers to open a checking account; low income customers also need to encourage using other accounts available to them (e.g., savings accounts, investment accounts). When consumers have a working relationship with their financial institution, the consumers save more and start a diversified portfolio. Diversification enables minorities to obtain home ownership and start to working toward creating future wealth for themselves and their families (Seidman & Tescher, 2005).

According to the 2010 Census, 75% of the African American population gains occurred in the South from 2000 to 2010. Atlanta, Dallas, and Houston superseded other metropolitan cities in gains. The African American population dropped in cities to include: New York, Chicago, and Detroit   According to the 2010 census, one-third of the Asian-American population resides in Los Angeles, San Francisco, and New York City. Asian-Indians accounted for more growth in 63 of the 100 major metropolitan cities. Nearly 50% of Hispanic-Americans live in 10 of the largest metropolitan areas, and these 10 Metropolitan cities only account for 36% of the Hispanic-American growth over the last 10 years

(Frey, 2011). About one-third of the largest cities doubled in their Hispanic-American population. In two-thirds of these cities, Mexican-Americans contributed to most of the Hispanic growth (Frey, 2011).

Appelbaum (2012) reviewed data from the U.S. Federal Reserve Board Survey of Consumer Finances highlighted the median American family in 2010. The U.S. Federal Reserve Board Survey of Consumer Finances states the economic crisis left American families with less median wealth than in the early 1990s. This decline removed over 20 years of prosperity. A typical American family with net worth of $77,300 in 2010 was a reduction from $126,400 in 2007. Family income also experienced a decline in 2010. The average median income was $45,800 in 2010, which was less than average median income in 2007 of $49,600.

Cardenas and Kelley (2012) reviewed data retrieved from the 2010 census. Georgia is in the middle of a population boom. Georgia's population increased more than 18% from 2000 to 2010. Georgia is one of 13 states where minorities make up more than 40% of its population. Georgia has 44.1% non-White-American residents. From 2000 to 2009, Georgia's Hispanic-American population accounts for 23.2% of its population. African-Americans accounts for 31.5% of the state's population. Hispanic-Americans account for 8.8% of the state's population, and Asian-Americans accounts for 3.8% of Georgia's population.

The 2010 census identified the median income for African-Americans and Hispanic- Americans in Georgia was 61.5 % and 63.9% of the median income of White-Americans (Cardenas & Kelley, 2012). Nearly half of the Hispanic-Americans and approximately one-fifth of the African-Americans did not have any form of health insurance; compared to just 14% for White Americans. In 2010, 12% of African-Americans, 11.8% of Mixed-Race, 8.2% Hispanic-Americans and 6.1% of White-

Americans were unemployed in the state of Georgia (Cardenas & Kelley, 2012).

Focus on Data Analysis Methodology

The James (2013) study offers a comparative study on mortgage lending practices to minority borrowers in the Atlanta, Georgia, area. As the author, I chose this topic to research because I am a resident of an Atlanta suburb. I have lived in Atlanta for over 15 years, and am a real estate appraiser and real estate agent. Therefore, I have seen the effects of predatory lending firsthand in various communities in the Atlanta area.

The James (2013) study was a qualitative study that used the phenomenological research design. Legislation is in place to minimize these practices, but because of a lack of awareness, many minorities in Atlanta, Georgia, and other parts of America receive high interest rate loans and paying exorbitant amounts of upfront fees, balloon payments. The author has extensive knowledge about the subject matter because she lives in an Atlanta suburb, and has been a real estate professional for over 10 years as a Real Estate Agent, and as a Certified Residential Appraiser. The author knows firsthand what happens to neighborhoods when homes are foreclosed upon because the homeowner could not make the payments because of balloon payments and high interest rates.

Findings

The author of the James (2013) study interviewed nine African-American Agents, nine White-Americans, six Hispanic-Americans (2 Puerto Rican, 1 Cuban, 1 Mexican, and 2 Venezuelan) and six Asian-Americans (2 Vietnamese, 1 Laotian, 1 Korean, and 2 Asian Indians). There were 17 women and 13 men. Women's ages ranged from 26 to 60, and men's ages ranged from 29 to 55. During the face-to-face recorded interviews, participants were asked the same 15 questions. The questions were based upon the following research questions:

1. Regarding lending practices and homeowners insurance, do minorities know their rights?
2. Concerning showing homes for sale, do real estate agents tend to select areas according to the ethnic background of prospective homeowners?

The author conducted in-depth, semi-structured interviews with participants. The goal of this type of interviewing was to help foster and encourage participants to be more vocal and truthful about their experiences. *Semi-structured* refers to that the interviewer does not need to ask only the predetermined questions. The James (2013) study included an *interview protocol* with written instructions on conducting the interview which included the process of *self-disclosure* to avoid bias. This self-disclosure was important because the author is a real estate agent and certified residential appraiser. She also has owned 16 rental properties during the same time period of when predatory lend and subprime loans were the main types of loans being funded by minorities. The author is also African American.

In the James (2013) study, the findings for the three hypotheses were significant based upon the sample size of the 30 agents interviewed. For Hypothesis 1, the alternate hypotheses were accepted, "Minority homeowners having a lack of home insurance have made it difficult to obtain a home mortgage." For hypotheses 2, the null hypothesis was accepted, "Real estate agents tend to not show homes in certain areas because of the ethnic background of their borrowers". For hypothesis 3, the alternate hypothesis was accepted, "There are a large number of minority homebuyers that do not receive the best interest rate from their lenders Procedures". The running theme for this study was lack of awareness in the minority communities. Most of the agents believe that the minorities could benefit greatly from more education and having a better understanding of the three credit bureaus, as well as how they can hinder future hopes of homeownership.

Summary

Jourdain-Earl (2012) found that a *dual mortgage market* had emerged. White-Americans and Asian-American borrowers had more access to lower cost mortgages than both African-Americans and Hispanic-Americans did. When African American and Hispanic American borrowers do obtain a mortgage, they pay more on average to own or refinance their homes. Jourdain-Earl further stated that high costs of mortgage credit lead to African-American and Hispanic-Americans having lower homeownership rates and fewer opportunities to build generational wealth as their Asian-American and White-American counterparts. These costs lead to lower educational achievements and more unemployment. Jourdain-Earl noted that the higher cost loans that were made to minority borrowers were the cause of the high levels of loan defaults and foreclosures. These defaults and foreclosures also led to further disparities to access credit (Cooper, 2011).

The first hypothesis examined minority homeowner's awareness about obtaining homeowners insurance. Several themes were identified based upon how the agents responded. Some of the agents stated a lack of education on home insurance was an issue. Others stated minority clients did not understand the process. Some even stated clients needed to be guided systematically.

The second hypothesis examined if real estate agents only showed certain types to homes to certain ethnic groups. When asked, 'In your experience have you ever showed a home in an undesirable neighborhood because of your homebuyer's race or ethnic origin,' all 30 of the agents responded that they did not show homes in undesirable neighborhoods to their minority clients. Real estate agents could be fined and possibly have to surrender their license to their local Real estate commission board.

Hypothesis three dealt with whether minority home buyers receiving good interest rates from lenders. When asked, "What could be done, if anything, to make it easier for the homeowner to obtain those prime interest rates", there were five themes identified. Nearly half of the agents (12) stated more credit education was needed in minority communities about the importance of maintaining a good credit score. Other participants stated language support (information in their native language) was imperative. Others stated interest rate education, while some said an overview of financials and its importance to the lending process was important. Nearly 25% of the agents interviewed stated if their borrowers understood the entire process from the obtaining the mortgage, obtaining home insurance, maintain good credit rating would help minorities receive prime interest rates (James, 2013).

The James (2013) study support the findings of Cooper (2011) and others regard the disparities in lending practices in minority communities. Subprime loans and high default rates, in many ways have had a deleterious effect on the progress African Americans and Hispanic-Americans have made in the last 20 years. Homeownership brings a sense of pride in one's community, and ultimately yields to generational wealth. Homeownership dwindling in minority communities will minimize the opportunities of generational wealth.

Conclusion

The focus of the James (2013) study was to identify any disparities amongst minority borrowers in regards to homeowners insurance and obtaining prime interest rate loans from the perspective of local real estate agents in the Atlanta Metropolitan area. The James study took an in depth look of the impacts of predatory lending through the viewpoint of local real estate agents in the Atlanta, Georgia metropolitan area. Other research has been conducted on the borrowers that were impacted by predatory lending practices. The James study captured a theme amongst the 30 agents interviewed. The theme was lack of education and awareness is why minorities has been negatively impacted by the home value declines in the mid-2000s.

References

Appelbaum, B. (2012). *Family net worth drops to level of early 90s, Feds say.* Retrieved from

http://www.nytimes.com/2012/06/12/business/economy/family-net-worth-drops-to-level-of-early-90s-fed-says.html?_r=0

Bailey, N. (Summer 2005). Predatory Lending: The New Face of Economic Injustice. Retrieved from http://www.americanbar.org/publications/human_rights_magazine_home/human_rights_vol32_2005/summer2005/hr_summer05_predator.html

Cárdenas, V., & Kelley, A. (2012, March). The top 10 things you should know about Georgia's demographic changes and immigration politics: a look at the state's emerging communities of color before the republican primary. Retrieved from http://www.americanprogress.org/issues/race/news/2012/03/02/11191/the-top-10-things-you-should-know-about-georgias-demographic-changes-and-immigration-politics

Champagne, D. M. (2012, March 7). U.S. senate hears about impacts of predatory lending. *Daily Record. Retrieved From* http://www.dailyrecord.com/

Cooper, K. (2011, February 9). New analysis: home mortgages to minorities plummet by 62 percent. *America's Wire, News Report.* Retrieved from missing information

Creswell, J. (2007). *Qualitative inquiry and research design: Choosing among five approaches* (2nd ed.). Thousand Oaks, CA: Sage.

Frey, W. (2011, August). The new metro minority map: regional shifts in hispanics, asians, and Blacks from census 2010. Retrieved from http://www.brookings.edu/research/papers/2011/08/31-census-race-frey

Georgia Department of Community Affairs. (2008). Neighborhood

Stabilization Program: Substantial Amendment for the State of Georgia Retrieved from http://www.dca.ga.gov/communities/CDBG/programs/documents/NSP_Final_Amendment.pdf

Kalil, A., & Wightman, P. (2009). Parental job loss and children's educational attainment in black and white middle class families. National Poverty Center Working Paper.

Retrieved   from   http://www.npc.umich.edu/publications/working_ papers/?publication_id=171&

Krivo, L. J., & Kaufman, R. L. (2004). Housing and wealth inequality: Racial-ethnic differences in home equity in the United States. *Demography, 41*, 585–605.doi: 10.1353/dem.2004.0023

Pew Charitable Trusts. (2008). *Defaulting on the dream: States respond to America's foreclosure crisis.* Retrieved from http://www.pewtrusts.org/ uploadedFiles/wwwpewtrustorg/Reports/subprime_mortgages/defaulting_ on_the_dream.pdf

RealtyTrac. (2009). *2009 U.S. Foreclosure Market Report.* Retrieved from http://www.realtytrac.com

Schwartztol, L. (2011). Predatory lending: wall street profited, minority families paid the price. Retrieved from http://www.aclu.org/blog/racial-justice/ predatory-lending-wall- street-profited-minority-families-paid-price

Shapiro, T. M. (2004). *The hidden cost of being African-American: How wealth perpetuates inequality.* Oxford, UK: Oxford University Press.

Tyuse & Birkenmaier, (2006) Promoting homeownership for the poor: Proceed with caution. *Race, Gender, & Class, 13*(3-4), 295-310.doi: 10.2307/ i40078746

Wyly, E.K., Atia, M., Foxcroft, H., Hammel, D.J., Phillips-Watts, K., & Wyly, E.K. (2006). American home: Predatory mortgage capital and neighborhood spaces of race and class exploitation in the United States. DOI: 10.1111/j.0435-3684.2006.00208

About the Author...

Dr. Coleen M James is originally from the beautiful island of Antigua. She currently resides in Cobb County, Georgia. Dr. Coleen holds several accredited degrees; a Bachelor of Science (BS) in Communications from the Florida State University; a Master of Business Administration (MBA) from Kennesaw State University; and a Doctorate of Business Administration (DBA) from Argosy University.

Dr. Coleen is an Adjunct Professor at Strayer University, Saint Leo University, and Colorado State University: Global. She is approved to teach business, management, and marketing courses. She enjoys the interaction with students, striving to provide a pathway to academic excellence within the classroom. She is a member of the U.S. Distance Learning Association (USDLA) and Delta Sigma Theta Sorority.

Dr. Coleen is President and CEO of CMJ Appraisals and Investments, a real estate appraisal company. She holds professional licenses in real estate and is a certified residential appraiser. She is also an active member in her local church.

To reach Dr. Coleen M. James for information on consulting services, please e-mail: jamesc@bellsouth.net

CHAPTER 6

Strategic and Scenario Planning Using Delphi:
Long-term and Rapid Planning Using the Genius of Crowds

By Dr. Elmer Hall & Dr. Edgar A. Jordan

The Delphi Method is a technique for gathering expert information, in multiple rounds of learning, to analyze a specific issue and make informed conclusions. Of the many applications, including dissertation research and strategic-scenario planning, some of the best uses of the Delphi technique are neglected. This article focuses on aspects of planning including how and when planning teams might be engaged. In the normal planning processes – especially horizon, scenario, sustainability, Total Quality management (TQM), and disaster recovery planning (DRP) – triggers are identified to signal that the scenario is about to happen, or has already occurred. Once the trigger has been tripped, teams must be assembled to review continuity plans and to initiate action. Delphi is a useful planning tool at all stages: up front in the scenario planning process, as well as, after the trigger has been tripped. Teams, including Delphi panels, can be used in rapid planning as well. The genius of crowds can be engaged during the planning process and even in the face of an emergency. But for these teams to work most effectively, the mechanism for engaging, or re-engaging, the team has to be well developed

(Crowdsourcing, 2013). Even in academic research, there could be – and should be – an opt-in mechanism for reengaging the team.

Strategic and Scenario Planning Using Delphi: Long-Term and Rapid Planning Using the Genius of Crowds

Long-term planning such as horizon, scenario, and sustainability planning are very powerful tools that often use Delphi research methods. After the Great Recession of 2007-2009, a McKinsey study found that executives were much more likely to do scenario planning than prior to 2007 (Dye, Sibony, & Viguerie, 2009; Hall, 2009a). The purpose of this article is to examine some of the best practices of using Delphi for planning and for academic research. Covered in this article are variations of the types of nominal group and Delphi studies; types of planning or studies that could use Delphi; the composition of (potential) nominal groups; the aspects of triggers and planning that could use new or revived Delphi team analysis; and, follow-on academic research associated with a Delphi dissertation study. This article focused on extending the Delphi group learning process beyond where it typically leaves off. What are ways to maintain contact with the original group so that further research could be done on an *ad hoc* basis? What are ways of creating teams or reviving past teams in case of crisis?

An Overview of Delphi and Various Implementations

The RAND Corporation is a contracting firm that helped the U.S. government plan various scenarios during the cold war (Hall, 2009b; Lindstone & Turoff, 1975). The RAND created the Delphi Method that used experts and engaged them in multiple rounds of information gathering and feedback. The Delphi

Method minimizes many of the problems with using teams, such as *group think* (Straus, Parker, Bruce, & Dembosky, 2009). Because team members are anonymous, and they do not physically meet together, the chance of one person dominating the group and *group think* are minimized. Delphi creates an organized learning process where the results from the last round are presented with the comments and thoughts of the participants so that a final consensus can be reached, if possible.

Jordan, in 2010, found a growing use of the Delphi research, particularly in health and education related studies. In both of these disciplines, the Delphi method is often used to establish standards of care in the case of health related research (Ferri, Prince, Brodaty, & Fratiglioni, 2005; Finger, Cieza, Stoll, Stucki, & Huber, 2006; Gagliardi, Simunovic, Langer, Stern, & Brown, 2005; Keeney, Hasson, & McKenna, 2006; Schnyer, Conboy, Jacobson, McKnight, & Goddard, 2005) and teaching methodologies in the case of education related research (Champion, 2007; Dinnebeil, McInerney, & Hale, 2006). Apparently, the use of the Delphi method may be increasing in the social sciences; generally, the use of this method appears to be constant with time as evident from published dissertations.

Table 1 indicates the primary types of nominal group analysis and how the traditional Delphi Method compares to variations of this method are sometimes referred to as a *modified Delphi* study (Dalkey & Helmer, 1963; Hall, 2009b; Helmer & Dalkey, 1999). Note the traditional Delphi Method on the left and the modified Delphi on the right. The difference is that some aspect of the pure Delphi method is not adhered to; typically the main differences are that true experts are not necessary – maybe just informed people will suffice – or consensus is not required. The UCLA/ RAND approach is used for medical protocols in which the ideal result for a best practice treatment would be full consensus on the best, *most appropriate*, treatment given the evidence and experience of the doctors (Ferri, Prince, Brodaty, & Fratiglioni, 2005; Finger, Cieza, Stoll, Stucki, & Huber, 2006; Gagliardi, Simunovic, Langer, Stern, & Brown, 2005; Keeney, Hasson, & McKenna, 2006; Schnyer, Conboy, Jacobson, McKnight, & Goddard, 2005).

Table 1:
Typical Uses of Various Implementations of Delphi-Type Research

Category	Traditional Delphi	Nominal Group Technique	UCLA/RAND Appropriateness	Modified Delphi
Number of participants?	Few, maybe 5 to 20.	Few, maybe 5 to 20.	Few, maybe 5 to 20.	Group, maybe 12 thru 50; multiple groups?
Level of expertise?	Experts	Experts, usually	Experts	Knowledgeable, not necessarily expert
Industry?	Military, gov., competitive strategy	All industries	Medical treatment, to recommend a protocols	All industries.
Iterations?	2 or more, often 3	2 or more, usually 2	2 or more	1 or more
Anonymous?	Usually	No	Not necessarily	Usually
Meet together in one setting (virtually or physically)?	Usually not	Yes, one meeting	Usually	If necessary
Aim for one consensus?	Yes	Usually	Yes, one best protocol	Frequently not

Although the Delphi method is used in business, the frequency of its use is difficult to determine, since it is not published like academic studies. There are several areas of opportunity in which Delphi could be used in the planning processes. In all cases, when the teams end, there usually is no plan to reengage the panel.

Scenario Planning and Event Triggers
Scenario planning is a process of looking at the future and attempting to identify major deflection points (Chung & Choi,

2013; Kahane, 2012; Tidd & Bessant, 2009). Typical planning looks shorter term and aims for best case, worst case, and most-likely case of the future, all represent the "official view" of the future (Millett 2003; Chermack 2004). Scenario planning aims for viable alternative futures, circumstances where the official view, is no longer viable (Piiraninen, Kortelainen, Elfvengren, & Touminen, 2010). Figure 1 indicates the official view of the future and two identified scenarios, Scenario A should be advantageous for the firm and Scenario Z should be very difficult for the firm and its industry. Technology and disruptive innovation are always good candidates for scenarios (Jordan, 2010a, 2010b; Rikkonen, Kaivo-oja & Aakkula, 2006). Geopolitical events and government can form the basis of scenarios. A non-sustainable activity, if perpetuated, is certain to result in some scenario, like the ugly Recession of 2007-2009 that resulted from the financial and housing bubble collapse (Hall, 2010b; Hall & Hinkelman, 2013; Hall & Knab, 2012).

Hall and Hinkelman (2013) said this about the scenario planning process:

> Executives of organizations, especially in the USA, tend to plan for one "official view" of the future. They are focused on surviving the profitability battle of today, leaving the longer-term wars of the uncertain future – wars that may not even occur – for another day (and for someone else). Types of planning for such events as ice storms, hurricanes, terrorist attacks, market crashes, housing bubbles and category killer patents by competitors are often neglected. In the present method for most organizations, the strategies developed assume a future with conditions that are similar to the past. When conditions change dramatically, the plan is broken. *Strategic planning that includes the use of*

scenarios planning will result in strategies, goals, tactics and action items that provide more flexibility and adaptability. (p. 160)

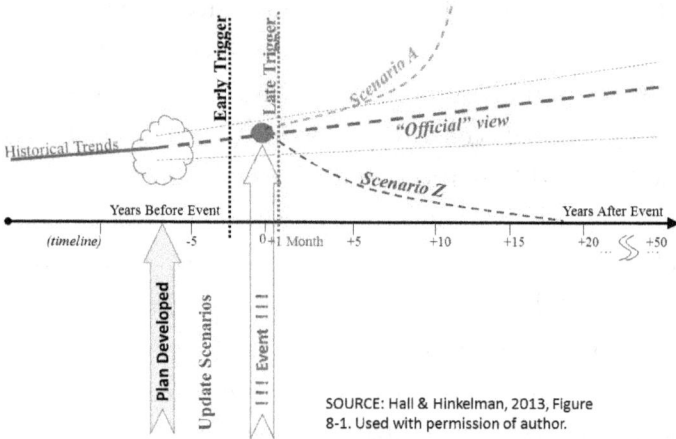

SOURCE: Hall & Hinkelman, 2013, Figure 8-1. Used with permission of author.

Figure 1. Scenario Views of the Future

Note that often multiple possible triggers indicate a scenario might be occurring. *Signals and signposts* are terms used by Royal Dutch Shell, PLC, the original developer of scenario planning, within their framework (Royal Dutch Shell, 2013). Some triggers might be early warning; and they might even be false warnings. Other triggers might be observed after the scenario has already begun.

A good example of the need for well thought through scenario planning and trigger identification can be found when considering disruptive innovation. In the late 1980s, Anderson and Tushman (1990) identified a cyclic phenomenon, particularly in the glass making industry that represented a considerable disruption to the industry with the advent of a new technology. Christensen (1997) later expanded on this work to include industries emerging in electronics industry. Dubbed *disruptive innovation*, Christensen followed the rise and fall of whole segments of the computer industry that was dominated at the high end by International Business Machines (IBM) so-called main frames, and the low end by Digital Electronics Company (DEC) with so-called minicomputers. When IBM introduced what has become known as the personal computer, or PC, the computing landscape completely changed.

As Christensen (1997) observed, when a disruptive innovation is introduced in the marketplace, the new technology usually performs poorly and is often more expensive than the technology the innovation eventually displaces. For this reason, the industry leader's best interests are not well served to invest in the emerging technology. In fact, the industry leader would have to divert scarce resources from profitable efforts to engage in maturing the emerging technology – at a loss to company owners and investors. The result is, once the emerging technology begins to mature, the industry leader will be driven out of the marketplace, at least for the applicable product line. For these reasons it was the logical outcome for DEC to be driven into bankruptcy with the advent of IBM's PC. Dell and Hewlett-Packard introduced disruptive manufacturing techniques that eventually drove IBM completely from the low-end computer market altogether. Likewise, Xerox is no longer in the copier business because of the advent of digital copying technologies. It is Christensen's (1997) thesis that these industry upheavals were the natural outcome of disruptive innovation.

One of the questions that such disruptive technologies brings to mind is how an industry leader would avoid the fate of the IBMs, DECs, Xeroxes, of the world? With well thought through scenario planning, the advent of the applicable disruptive technologies may have been anticipated. In their book Christensen and Raynor (2003) suggested an organizational structure that would allow various ideas to *find legs,* so to speak, as concepts competed against each other for viability. What was not discussed was how these various competing ideas might be identified in the first place. Recent work sought to do just that with the semiconductor manufacturing industry using a modified Delphi approach (Jordan, 2010b). This study recruited the Delphi panel participants by the use of personal invitation on the social media website LinkedIn. The study took place in three rounds addressing the following questions: when might a technology emerge that would replace the current material used as a semiconductor; what might that technology be; what leadership approach would be most likely to facilitate the emergence of the new technology; and what organizational structure would best be suited for that emergence?

The Delphi panel in the Jordan (2010b) study converged on findings that were both interesting and suggest wider applicability regarding scenario planning. The panel found that a technology to replace silicon dioxide would most likely emerge sometime during the next 30 years. Jordan's panel found the emerging technology would mostly likely be biologic, probably protein based. The panel found the leadership method best suited to facilitate the emergence of this new technology would likely be transformational. Finally, the panel also found that the organizational structure that would be most effective in facilitating the emergence was a meritocracy. Unlike earlier work (Christensen & Raynor, 2003) the Jordan (2010b) study provided a specific framework within which scenario planning and triggers could be addressed. As suggested in Figure 1, a Delphi method similar to that used in the Jordan study would be useful in establishing what event should be addressed for a particular scenario, when that event might occur, and what the early and late triggers might be in anticipation of the event might be to achieve a favorable trajectory.

Types of Planning and Triggers for Scenario Events

Although there are many applications of Delphi, the existing areas of planning for an organization are ideal to consider how this technique might be used. The most common planning areas are shown in Table 2 along with the trigger and planning team components associated with Delphi-types of research.

Table 2
Types of Planning and Triggers Created or Activate

Type of Planning	Trigger Created?	Panel/Team Follow-up
Horizon planning. Horizon planning, including scenario and sustainability planning, is the process of developing long term plans (Hall & Hinkelman, 2013). This is not a 5-year plan; it is 25 years, at least. For a power company, it may take decades to bring new plants online, so horizon plans will be 75 to 100 years. Scenario planning can use Delphi, and probably should use Delphi methods initially. Figure 1 shows how scenario plans could be developed, combined with triggers that indicate that a scenario is starting to happen, or that the scenario has happened.	*Triggers would be developed* within long-term planning to indicate that a scenario is happening or could start soon.	*Maybe permanent team.* Scenarios are reviewed periodically. Team may become part of the action team associated with triggers.
Total Quality Management (TQM). TQM programs such as ISO9000 and Six Sigma are an integral part of larger companies and all manufacturing firms. This Plan-Do-Check-Act cycle works well on the production line. When the process moves out of the normal and into a new area, say sustainability, the initial measures and metrics are often non-existent; maybe this new process analysis involves the whole supply chain, or all producers in the industry. A Delphi process might be a way to launch into this new area, helping identify what should be measured, and providing the first informed estimates of how critical those factors are.	*Triggers should be developed* within the TQM framework to determine when a process is *out of control.*	*Operational-level team,* but maybe the original team might continue to be involved in measuring performance.
Continuity Plans (including DRP). DRP plans are usually associated with the office or factory to recover from a catastrophic event like hurricanes or tornados. A continuity plan should include procedures for the failures of key business partners and the supply chain. Critical partners will usually include the utility companies with power, water, and gas.	*Activated by Triggers!*	*Pre-defined team.* Teams are ready for action and mechanism is in place.
Triggered Event Actions and Planning. A trigger has been tripped because of a scenario signal or an out-of-control process; engaging a pre-defined rapid response team is necessary, maybe critical. If additional planning is required, a Delphi-like team might be needed, but there will not necessarily be time to select and coordinate a team. A better solution might be to reassemble the past Delphi team that helped with the creation of the scenarios or contingencies?	*Triggered event*	*Pre-defined team.* Triggered event may not have the team already created.
Ad hoc. An *ad hoc* team would be created without any pre-planning, maybe for competitive purposes or a looming, but unique, disaster. Although something triggers the requirement for the team, no pre-defined event or trigger initiated the activation. Team must be created.	*Ad hoc* would not have pre-defined triggers.	*No pre-defined team.* *Ad hoc* probably does not have plans.
Academic Research. Delphi is an excellent tool to do academic research in areas that otherwise would be impractical or impossible to research. Often finding informed or expert participants will allow for in-depth research where it would otherwise take two studies or not even be possible with the constraints of a dissertation. The results are often provided directly back to the participants as a courtesy for their participation. The nature of the study generally limits the ability of the doctoral candidate from reengaging the panel after completion.	*No triggers.*	*No provision to reengage the panels.*

As the review of how and where Delphi is often used, it becomes apparent that possessing the ability to quickly create teams and the ability to revive past teams has distinct advantages. The advantages of using past teams is not only the speed of engaging them, but also the avoidance of the problems associated with someone new having only a superficial view of the interrelatedness of issues and analysis from the prior panel rounds. The reliance of only the past team members may create a blind space of a different more current perspective. Thus, maybe the best approach would be some mix of prior and new panel members with (statistical) controls to identify any disparities between them.

Groups and the Genius of Crowds

Hall (2010a) demonstrated how impressive the engagement of crowds can be on a perpetual basis such as Wikipedia for planning and innovation. "Underlying the effective use of Delphi techniques is the effective use of groups to come up with better decisions than an individual would" (Hall, 2010a, p. 9). Surowiecki (2004) refers to this as *the wisdom of crowds* and *collective wisdom*. Techniques used by Delphi help make the best use of team analysis and decision-making (Hall, 2010a; Straus, et al., 2009). The most widely used and most successful collaborative tool of all time is Wikipedia (Hall, 2010a, Appendix A: Group Collaboration using Wikipedia). This great wiki truly demonstrates the genius of crowds with an effective way to tap millions of contributors and editors.

The nature of the groups formed for a Delphi-type study depends on multiple factors. Probably the most important is the level of confidentiality needed. Because the team is typically anonymous, even after the last round, that may not be so much of an issue. The results might be confidential, suggesting that maybe only employees and confidential contractors might be considered.

A good way to look at the openness of the study is to compare it to the security within the firm on the network. From most confidential to least confidential and secure would be:

- Local area network (LAN). Employees only, and may be trusted contractors.
- Wide area network (WAN). LAN plus employees from other regions and divisions.
- Extra net. Information that is available to employees as well as customers and business partners.
- Worldwide web (Internet). This means that anyone, anywhere, can get access.

Employees can be instructed to participate, but outside the organization, enticing volunteers is required. Other issues pertain to publishing and disseminating the results of the study, which may have sections less confidential.

A similar aspect of groups is how to identify prospective panelists. Even for employees a skills repository – a common baseline of knowledge – is needed to select internal *experts*. If the study is open to the world, there are usually ways to find people with certain interest in online forums (e.g., Facebook or LinkedIn) and ways to find people with certain degrees or certifications (e.g., patent attorneys or CPA accountants). Jordan (2010b) linked in to LinkedIn, for example, but other social media could be used such as Facebook and Twitter.

There might be legal restrictions to doing a Delphi study. For example, United States' antitrust laws prohibit the companies in an industry from openly discussing prices, and consequently collusive behaviors such as *price fixing* (U.S. Federal Trade Commission, 2010). This legal framework has the inconvenience of restricting companies in high-concentration industries (like oligopolies) from addressing industry-wide issues like safety and sustainability. Hall (2010a) argued that BP missed the boat before, during, and after the Deepwater Horizon disaster in the Gulf of Mexico. An industry-wide organization has since been created to handle safety and recovery.

Academic Research Using Delphi

Hall (2009b) discussed performing academic research using Delphi. Hall (2009b) described reasons a Delphi study would be appropriate for qualitative or mixed research. Delphi is usually considered qualitative research, typically focusing first on descriptive analysis. If the subsequent rounds do sufficient quantitative analysis such as correlation, the study would be characterized as mixed method (Hall, 2009b). Since 1970, 1.5 out of every 1,000 dissertations submitted to UMI/ProQuest are Delphi studies (or about 0.15%); however, these kinds of studies are used much more frequently in graduate-level research in business, education, and the social sciences. As doctoral candidates are conducting the research on their dissertations, they are focused on finishing their dissertations (and their doctorate), not on any possible research after *doctordom*. One thing that seems to be missing is the ability to reengage the team. Candidates usually offer to provide the results as a courtesy, but that is all. If a disaster occurs, or simple follow-on research would be desirable, the doctoral candidate does not typically have the mechanism in place to reach out to that group again. In fact, they are often ethically restricted from using these participants, and the results, for anything other than the original research. An informed consent form, for example, would typically ask participants for permission associated with the original dissertation research, nothing more. Opportunities for follow-on research and publishing could be missed.

The question becomes how to engage a panel for yet another round or so, after the original research has been concluded. Doctoral researchers have a special situation; they will need to create an invited partnership with panel members. This new opt-in relationship could be optimal for passing on key findings from the dissertation, as promised. It could be used for other things, as well. Just a couple ways to do this would be via Twitter, a Facebook page, Google + circle, and a LinkedIn forum (Crowdsourcing, 2013; Meek, 2013). Perhaps a blog would work well, something to provide ongoing information about the dissertation topic to members (and followers). Doctoral researchers would still need to respect the explicit and the implicit nature of the participants' agreement to participate in the original research; they only agreed to the original study, any further engagement with them would be a new, voluntary relationship, and should be well communicated.

Extending Delphi to the Nth Round

One key step in the Delphi process is assembling the team, especially in the case of scenario planning; there has been extensive thinking about unusual circumstances and the possible triggers for them. Scenarios will always include disasters, although that could be handled through a disaster recovery plan, and might not require the reengagement of a Delphi team. There are many advantages to keeping the original scenario teams on speed-dial, so to speak. Reengaging teams would be faster, and the team could be more productive, more quickly. By planning the team at the same time the triggers are developed, it is possible to have all of the additional support ready to react when a trigger has been tripped. This next round, long after the Delphi study has been completed that developed the scenarios, might be called the *Nth round*.

Associated with this Nth round would be the entire process of monitoring the triggers. The team itself would receive periodic notices of the status of triggers. As well, the scenarios and DRP plans would be reviewed periodically, typically annually. At that time certain scenarios might be retired and new scenarios developed. The triggers and the team engagement protocols would be reviewed for the scenarios to remain active.

Conclusion

Scenario planning is vital to the future success of any organization. Many specific scenarios, events, and triggers exist that must be understood for the organization to achieve a favorable trajectory after the event occurs. The central goal of scenario planning is identifying what those events might be and how it might be understood when an event is about to occur. The event in question might be catastrophic such as destruction resulting from a terrorist attack or a major earthquake. The event might appear subtly such as an emerging technology that could prove to be disruptive in the sense that Christensen suggests (1997). The spectrum of the possible events that might occur must be narrowed to those that are plausible and have the most potential impact.

We suggest considering Delphi, modified to fit the particular circumstances. Delphi is ideally suited to provide the mechanism to approach long-term and scenario planning in a structured, rigorous way. Even continuous improvement programs (TQM) could benefit from Delphi in some cases, as well as clear trigger mechanisms. This rigor makes Delphi most valuable. The details of each event, and the types of teamwork needed to addresses that event, will vary. Delphi is highly malleable and lends itself to application across the spectrum of potential events. However, for any team to be effective after a sign-post has been reached or a trigger been tripped, it is essential that the team can be quickly assembled, in a rapid response approach.

Even in academia, many types of studies – not just Delphi – use experts, and a mechanism could be established to re-engaging the original sample population. In cases of health, safety, and emergencies, such a link might be even advised. This has to be done carefully, however, probably with an opt-in mechanism completely separate from the dissertation or thesis.

The use of groups and the genius of crowds is a mathematical inflection point in learning, growing and decision making. Those who leverage the support of informed people, employ them wisely, and engage them rapidly, are going to be successful where others fail. These innovative organizations will help solve the overarching problems of a hot, flat and crowded world (Friedman, 2009). They will be able to profitably engage the triple bottom-line of sustainability with a win, win, win (Hall, & Knab, 2012). They will be refractive and ready to deflect to a new course, and they will have the triggers in place to identify when a new trajectory is imminent.

References

Anderson, P., & Tushman, M. (1990). Technological discontinuities and dominant designs: A cyclical model of technological change. *Administrative Science Quarterly, 35*, 604-633. doi: 10.2307/2393511

Champion, P. A. (2007). Equity vs. excellence: A Delphi study examining the future ramifications of NCLB on gifted education. *Dissertations Abstracts International: Section A. Humanities and Social Sciences, 68*(07), 209A-250. Retrieved from: http://catalogue.nla.gov.au/Record/2373510

Chermack, T. J. (2004). A theoretical model of scenario planning. *Human Resource Development Review, 3(4)*, 301-325. doi: 10.1177/1534484304270637

Christensen, C. M. (1997). *The innovator's dilemma: When new technologies cause great firms to fail.* Boston, MA: Harvard Business School Press.

Christensen, C. M., & Raynor, M. E. (2003). *The innovator's solutions: Creating and sustaining successful growth.* Boston, MA: Harvard Business School Press.

Chung, D., & Choi, B. (2013). Just-in-time scheduling under scenario-based uncertainty. *Asia-Pacific Journal of Operational Research, 30*, G1-g14. doi: 10.1142/S0217595912500558

Crowdsourcing. (2013, June 18). In *Wikipedia, The Free Encyclopedia.* Retrieved June 18, 2013, from: http://en.wikipedia.org/w/index.php?title=Crowdsourcing&oldid=560441664

Dalkey, N., & Helmer, O. (1963). An experimental application of the Delphi method to the use of experts. *Management Science, 9*, 458-467. doi: 10.1287/mnsc.9.3.458

Dinnebeil, L., McInerney, W., & Hale, L. (2006). Understanding the roles and responsibilities of itinerant ECSE teachers through Delphi research. *Topics in Early Childhood Special Education, 26*, 153-166. doi: 10.1177/02711214060260030301

Dye, R., Sibony, O., & Viguerie, S. P. (2009, April). Strategic planning: Three tips for 2009. *McKinsey Quarterly*, 3-27. Retrieved from:http://www.mckinseyquarterly.com

Ferri, C. P., Prince, M., Brodaty, C., & Fratiglioni, L. (2005). Global prevalence of dementia: A Delphi consensus study. *The Lancet*, *366*, 2112 - 2117. Retrieved from: http://www.thelancet.com/

Finger, M. E., Cieza, A., Stoll, J., Stucki, G., & Huber, E. O. (2006). Identification of intervention categories for physical therapy, based on the international classification of functioning, disability, and health: A Delphi exercise. *Physical Therapy*, *86*, 1203-1220. Retrieved from: http://ptjournal.apta.org/

Friedman, T. (2009). Hot, flat, and crowded: Why we need a green revolution--and how it can renew America. New York, NY: Farrar, Straus, and Giroux.

Gagliardi, A. R., Simunovic, M., Langer, B., Stern, H., & Brown, A. D. (2005). Development of quality indicators for colorectal cancer surgery, using a 3-step modified Delphi approach. *Canadian Journal of Surgery*, *48*, 441-451. Retrieved from: http://www.cma.ca/cjs

Hall, E. (2009a). Strategic planning in times of extreme uncertainty. In C. A. Lentz (Ed.), *The refractive thinker: An anthology of higher learning* (pp. 41-57). Las Vegas, NV: The Refractive Thinker Press.

Hall, E. (2009b). The Delphi primer: Doing real-world or academic research using a mixed-method approach. In C. A. Lentz (Ed.), *The refractive thinker: Vol. 2: Research Methodology*, (pp. 3-27). Las Vegas, NV: The Refractive Thinker Press.

Hall, E. (2010a). Innovation out of turbulence: Scenario and survival plans that utilizes groups and the wisdom of crowds. In C. A. Lentz (Ed.), *The refractive thinker: Vol. 5.: Strategy in innovation* (pp. 1-20). Las Vegas, NV: The Refractive Thinker Press.

Hall, E. (2010b). Lessons of recessions: Sustainability education and jobs may be the answer. *Journal of Sustainability and Green Management*. *1*(1). Jacksonville, FL: Academic and Business Research Institute. Retrieved from: http://www.aabri.com/OC2010Manuscripts/OC10079.pdf

Hall, E. B., & Hinkelman, R. M. (2013). *Perpetual Innovation™: Guide to strategic planning, patent commercialization and enduring competitive advantage, Version 2.0.* Morrisville, NC: LuLu Press.

Hall, E., & Knab, E. F. (2012). Social irresponsibility provides opportunity for the win-win-win of Sustainable Leadership. In C. A. Lentz (Ed.), *The refractive thinker: Vol. VII Social responsibility* (pp. 197-220). Las Vegas, NV: The Refractive Thinker® Press.

Helmer, O., & Dalkey, N. (1999, Spring). The modified Delphi technique: A rotational modification. *Journal of Vocational and Technical Education, (15)*2. Retrieved from: http://scholar.lib.vt.edu/ejournals/JVTE/

Jordan, E. A. (2010 a). The next big disruptive innovation: Can you imagine a world without Intel? . In C. A. Lentz (Ed.), *The refractive thinker: Vol. V.: Strategy in innovation* (pp. 59-76). Las Vegas, NV: The Refractive Thinker® Press.

Jordan, E. A. (2010b) *The semiconductor industry and emerging technologies: A study using a modified Delphi method.* University of Phoenix, ProQuest, UMI Dissertations Publishing, 2010. 3442759

Kahane, A. (2013). Transformative scenario planning: Changing the future by exploring alternatives. *Strategy & Leadership, 40,* 19-23. doi:10.1108/78571211257140

Keeney, S., Hasson, F., & McKenna, H. (2006). Consulting the oracle: Ten lessons from using the Delphi technique in nursing research. *Journal of Advanced Nursing, 53,* 205 -212. doi: 10.1111/j.1365-2648.2006.03716.x

Linstone, H. A., & Turoff, M. (1975). *The Delphi method: Techniques and applications.* Reproduction electronically in 2002. Retrieved from: http://www.is.njit.edu/pubs/delphibook/

Meek, T. (2013, June 6). Crowdsourcing: Great for tour business (A handy primer). *Forbes.* Retrieved from: http://www.forbes.com/sites/netapp/2013/06/06/crowdsourcing-for-business/

Millett, S. M. (2003). The future of scenarios: Challenges and opportunities. *Strategy & Leadership, 31(2)*, 16-24. Retrieved from: http://www.regent.edu/acad/global/publications/jsl/home.htm

Piiraninen, K., Kortelainen, S., Elfvengren, K., & Touminen, M. (2010). A scenario approach for assessing new business concepts. *Management Research Review, 33*, 635-655.. doi:10.1108/014091710110500244

Rikkonen, P., Kaivo-oja, J., & Aakkula, J. (2006). Delphi expert panels in the scenario-based strategic planning of agriculture. *Foresight: The Journal of Futures Studies, Strategic Thinking and Policy, 8(1)*, 66-81. doi: 10.1108/14636680610647156

Schnyer, R. N., Conboy, L. A., Jacobson, E., McKnight, P., & Goddard, T. (2005). Development of a Chinese medicine assessment measure: An interdisciplinary approach using the Delphi method. *Journal of Alternative and Complementary Medicine, 11*, 1005-1013. Retrieved from: http://www.liebertpub.com/overview/journal-of-alternative-and-complementary-medicine-the/26/

Royal Dutch Shell, PLC. (2013). Shell scenarios. Retrieved from: http://www.shell.com/global/future-energy/scenarios

Surowiecki, J. (2004). *The wisdom of crowds: Why the many are smarter than the few and how collective wisdom shapes business, economies, societies, and nations.* New York, NY: Doubleday.

Straus, S. G., Parker, A. M., Bruce, J. B., & Dembosky, J. W. (2009, April). *The group matters: A review of the effects of group interaction on processes and outcomes in analytic Teams.* RAND Corporation. Document: WR580. Retrieved from: http://www.rand.org/pubs/working_papers/2009/RAND_WR580.pdf

Tidd, J., & Bessant, J. (2009). *Managing innovation: Integrating technology, market and organizational change.* West Sussex, UK: John Wiley & Sons.

U.S. Federal Trade Commission. (2010, January 6). FTC guide to the antitrust laws. Retrieved June 28, 2013,

from: http://www.ftc.gov/bc/antitrust/

THE REFRACTIVE THINKER®

About the Author...

Dr. Elmer Hall *helps individuals and organizations plan for success that sustainably balances wellness and wealth.*

Dr. Elmer holds several accredited degrees: BA and MBA from the University of South Florida; and a Doctorate of International Business Administration (DIBA) from Nova Southeastern University. For 25 years, he taught business classes at the undergraduate and graduate levels at several Florida universities. He is a Facilitator and Dissertation Mentor for the University of Phoenix. His "real" education, however, is from his personal entrepreneurial ventures and those of clients.

Dr. Elmer is the President of Strategic Business Planning Company (www.SBPlan.com), doing strategic consulting for startups and existing ventures. He has also been interim Sustainability Officer and chair of a business incubator. Major clients: IBM, Ryder, NextEra (FP&L), and Burger King (Diageo).

Publications/Seminars are on survival/scenario, sustainability in business and education, innovation, economic development, patent planning and Delphi Method research. With Robert 'Bob' M. Hinkelman, Dr. Elmer authored *Perpetual Innovation™: A Guide to Strategic Planning, Patent Commercialization and Enduring Competitive Advantage* and also the *Patent Primer*. Look for version 2.0 of each at http://www.lulu.com/spotlight/SBPlan/. SBP has developed the Commercialization of Patent Assets, COMPASS®, process for intellectual property (IP) management (www.IPplan.com).

Blogs: http://www.SustainZine.com and
http://ipzine.blogspot.com/
Twitter @ SBPlan
To reach Dr. Elmer please e-mail: Elmer@SBPlan.com

About the Author...

Dr. Edgar A. Jordan resides in the village of Midlothian, Virginia, a suburb of Richmond. Dr. Ed holds several accredited degrees; a Bachelor of Science (BS) in Physics from Weber State University in Ogden, Utah; a Bachelor of Science (BS) in Electrical Engineering from the Naval Postgraduate School in Monterey California; a Master of Science (MS) in Engineering Acoustics also from the Naval Post Graduate School; and a Doctor of Business Administration from the School of Advanced Studies of the University of Phoenix. Dr. Ed's research focus is on technology and innovation management, in particular disruptive innovation; as well as organizational adaptation; and leadership theory.

Dr. Ed is President and CEO of 5 Rings Solutions, LLC; an enthusiastic consulting firm that focuses on acoustic system research and development, system integration, budget development, and at-sea sustainment, under contract to agencies in the Department of Defense. 5 Rings Solutions also provide services that enable organizations to maximize effectiveness, especially in the face of rapidly changing technological environments.

Dr. Ed has been elected to membership of Sigma Xi, The Scientific Research Society, and is an active member of the Acoustical Society of America and the Academy of Management.

To reach Dr. Ed please e-mail: eajordan@msn.com

CHAPTER 7

The Enlightened Pen: The Praxis Documentation and
Aesthetic Interpretation (PDAI) Research Model

by Dr. Bethany Mickahail and Dr. Kate Andrews

W hat research method propels enterprising dissertation students and seasoned academics to tap into original scholarship that results in a work that truly contributes to their study field and even influence the world? The Mickahail (2010) study highlighted in this chapter is a fresh hybrid research methodology, the Praxis Documentation and Aesthetic Interpretation (PDAI) model. The PDAI model chronicles the lived stories of individuals' experiences through oral history research techniques and poetic data display. The PDAI model derives the title from Mickahail's original inspiration for the research of social action, adapted from a qualitative hybrid research model presented in a dissertation by Mears (2005). Arendt (1958), an early 20th century philosopher of politics and architect of a theory of action, wrote in *The Human Condition* that everyday political action is an exercise in practical freedom and participatory democracy. Arendt was influenced by Aristotle's original notion of *praxis* or change practice. She molded the sage's idea into a modern concept of social action. For Arendt, praxis meant action that had culminated in implemented results within a participatory democracy.

For what ventures of research would this unique methodology be suitable? The answer is multi-faceted and limitless. Some examples include

- Studies in the arts, education, psychology, the sciences, and interdisciplinary studies.
- Major societal issues begging for discoveries that fuel the passion for research, such as studies chronicling major trends in society; school reform, civil rights, climate change, and technology, and inner city renewal.

These examples provide ideas from social change and changes having to do with environment and technology. As the world continues to change in all aspects (e.g., technologically, environmentally, population, politically) at a rampant pace, there are always opportunities for capturing the processes for future knowledge and lessons learned. The necessary elements to engage in exciting scholarly research are encompassed in the hybrid research PDAI model. Many forlorn dissertation students and crusty academics will find this methodology an escape from dissertation doldrums and a vehicle to research with intellectual possibilities!

Fire up the Research Engine!

When researchers consider the design and reporting of a proposed research project, the selection of a methodology is paramount to research progress. A strategic researcher will be quick to identify what exactly draws his or her own energy and enthusiasm. The thoughtful selection of a burning research topic and methodology focuses the wandering scholar through the massive effort and endless hours required to conduct the research and writing of a qualitative dissertation or research project.

The roadblock for many in writing a dissertation or research project is selecting the specific methodology most appropriate in answering the research question(s). To determine a qualitative research approach, scholars often concentrate on standard textual analysis of historical data, redacted results as well as standard qualitative focus groups, and individual open-ended interviews using standard coding analysis for the results. Researchers may also delve into other qualitative designs via a variety of existing models, such as case studies, narrative, ethnographic, and phenomenology approaches when contributing to the greater knowledge of their field of study.

The PDAI methodology emerged from Mickahail's (2010) fascination with the 20th century civil rights efforts, the subsequent societal transformation, and the endless energy of change makers. These ideas led Mickahail to the dissertation research topic, *Parents as Change Agents in their Schools and Communities.* Along with accessing a hybrid research model that used the method of oral history blended with Eisner's (1998) *enlightened eye* of educational criticism, Mickahail applied distinctive poetic representation through her *enlightened pen.* This poetic representation was the aesthetic instrument through which the data for the study was presented, analyzed, and displayed. This method led to the PDAI model, through which the powerful stories of parent change makers emerged. Mickahail illuminated the experiences of parents of children with autism by focusing on the original founding members of the parent organization: Families for Early Autism Treatment (FEAT). This small group forged groundbreaking advocacy efforts that ultimately benefited children with autism throughout the United States. The policy changers' motivational might, and the influence of their efforts, helped to anchor enduring change for children, families, and educational policy makers in their communities. The personal stories of those involved in establishing FEAT provide rare insights when placed in the context of the social, economic, educational, political, medical, and environmental repercussions of the innately modern crisis of autism. An aesthetic data display through poetic representation revealed the participant experiences. Through the interview to poetry analyzation, themes emerged to provide valuable lessons and perspectives through which others can be inspired to make profound changes in their schools, communities, and government policies. Mickahail determined the usefulness of process and steps of the PDAI model for others to capture the essence of the participants' experiences. The change processes highlighted and revealed in the Mickahail study can be applied to the societal, governmental, institutional, physiological, emotional, or psychological realms of research.

Research Design

The Mickahail study (2010) was conducted by creating and following the 4-continual step process of the PDAI model: developing a praxis framework, collecting and documenting oral history data, creating a poetic representation for aesthetic display and analysis, and determining resultant themes and findings revealed consistently throughout the poetic representation as indicated below. PDAI is a continual model because change never ceases but continues to grow, adjust, and refine into a cycle of transformation.

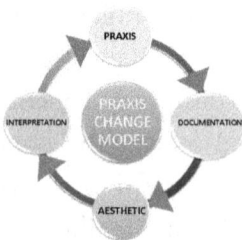

Figure 1. Indicates the components of the continual PDAI model (selecting a praxis oriented foundation for interview questions, conducting the actual interviews for documentation, creating poetic (aesthetic) representation for data analysis, and determining resultant themes to interpret into findings).

Developing a Framework

The first step in the initial stage of the PDAI model is developing a solid framework from which to collect data. Additionally, this step may have the researcher obtaining expert knowledge of the topic under investigation. In Mickahail's (2010) case, the research goal of recording the founding members' stories required a thorough investigation into the sweeping impact of autism.

In addition to using a qualitative research approach that requires intense researcher preparation for oral history interviews, the next step in the first stage of the PDAI model the researcher finalizes a framework for change as the foundation for developing the overreaching interview questions. Mickahail (2010) selected the existing eight-stage change model developed by Kotter (1996; 2006; 2008). To ensure consistency in the open-ended question format, Kotter's model served as a praxis framework from which to conduct the interviews for the research project. The interview questions addressed the overarching research question: What has been the experience of parents of children with autism who are also founders of FEAT? The first interview had specific questions based upon the first three stages of Kotter's change model: Stage 1: How did FEAT create a sense of urgency to help children with autism? Stage 2: How did you attract leaders and promote teamwork? Stage 3: How was the vision for FEAT created? How was it planned?

The second interview purposively centered on the next two stages in Kotter's (1996; 2006; 2008) model. The Stage 4 questions were "How did others become involved?" and "What attracted you?" Question used in Stage 5 were "What changes were a FEAT priority?" and "What risks were taken?" and "What new ideas were implemented?" The third interview utilized Kotter's stages 7 and 8 as the centering focus. Stage 7 questions asked, "What was learned?" and "Who or what was celebrated?" Stage 8 concluded with "How were FEAT's goals perpetuated and its successes anchored?"

> **Research tip:** Mickahail (2010) created interview questions utilizing the framework of Kotter's Change Model, which served as a way to structure data collection, through interviews, and methodology. However, future researchers may consider using a different framework for the participant interview questions depending on the research topic. For example, Kubler Ross' 5 Stages of Grief (Anaf et al., 2013) could be used to collect information on the change process related to loss. Another example would be to use the Bridges' Managing Transitions (2009) methodology associated with organizational and leadership challenges.

A third component of this stage is selecting the participants. Consistent with the expectations for a purposive, nonrandom sample, Mickahail (2010) had knowledge of the founding members of FEAT along with the privileged background and knowledge as a parent of a child with autism. As an advocate and skilled researcher, Mickahail obtained the trust of the participants, who were more likely to share openly about their exceptional experiences in developing a groundbreaking organization to advocate for children with autism. However, a researcher who is using the PDAI model does not have to have intimate, personal knowledge of the specific change process being investigated but in all cases must develop trust with the participants for open and honest oral history interview results. To finalize the framework for the data collection, the data and resultant interviews, the interview model of change was selected. The interview protocol was divided into three sessions to have information about aspects of the change process obtained during each interview.

Research tip: When selecting the interview sample of participants for the study. Ensure the interviewer and selected questions reflect a thorough study of the participants' personal story histories and related activities.

Collecting Oral History Data

Through the channel of oral history as the second stage of the PDAI model, a collection of rich and detailed data from the stories of the founding members emerged. Oral history provided these parents with a voice and a forum from which others may understand the strategies, tools, and techniques used to implement a program and to sustain a continuing legacy of advocacy and change. An appropriate method to build upon the strengths of traditional qualitative methods is the use of the collection of oral history. With the data obtained, Mickahail's extended the understanding and interpretation of how respondents construct the world around them through her *enlightened pen* (Glesne & Peshkin, 1992). Through oral history, the strengths of qualitative research are heightened with the method's focus on the perceptions, or stories of participants' views, experiences, and situations (Berg, 1989).

Oral history served the purpose of acknowledging and hearing the stories of those who have been traditionally marginalized. Specifically appropriate for the study of those dealing with disabilities and also other challenges, such as those coping with loss through war, tragedy, or as change makers, inventors, creators of art, and promoters of societal change, is the choice of capturing oral history of the change processes. The oral history method is used to chronicle the journey and stories of important contributors to society. Portelli (1997) wrote, "One of the two things that distinguishes oral history from other disciplines is the search for a connection between biography and history, between individual experience and the transformations of society" (p. 6).

Oral history was distinctively suited for this research about parent involvement, advocacy, and change.

Oral History: Validity and Reliability

The oral history method offers opportunities for data validation. Frisch (1990) wrote, "oral history is unique in that it creates its own documents, documents that are by definition explicit dialogues about the past, with the 'subject' necessarily triangulated between past experience and the present context of remembering" (p. 188). Validation opportunities are inherent to the oral history documentation process.

The employment of member checking addressed validity issues related to this type of qualitative research. The participants who had been interviewed were given the opportunity to read the interview answers to ensure that the information recorded was what they intended to convey. Reliability concerns addressed through thematic consistency, required the researcher to inquire of the participants if there was a consistency in the themes that emerged from the analyzed interview data. This inquiry process is the textual analysis within the next stage (Aesthetic) of the PDAI model. Additional questioning examined the data supported through the themes that surfaced from the original interviews by the researcher inquiring of each interviewee if the emerging themes supported his or her experience with FEAT. Thompson (2000) commented on the reliability of oral history through recording, as more reliable and accurate than a written record because the recording of oral history captures the exact words with social clues in the context of the participants of history.

Oral History: Data Collection

The data collection for this oral history featured in-depth interviews with five volunteer participants who were the founding members of FEAT in compliance with the oral history interview procedure guidelines (Berg, 1989; Ritchie, 2010; Seidman, 2006; University of California Berkeley, 2004; Yow, 1994). The oral history method utilized the format of a prolonged interview that involved the interviewer conducting multiple interviews with each participant (Denzin, 1970). Yow (1994) stated, "This is the great task of qualitative research and specifically oral history interviews: to reveal the meanings of lived experience" (p. 25). Grele (1985) presupposed that oral history be used to capture a conscious, critical account of history by the participants within historic events. In the pursuit of a more critical history, the Mickahail(2010) study extended and contributed to established oral historic research collections documenting the history of a specific branch of the diverse disability rights movement; autism.

To facilitate the emergence of significant meanings and the effectiveness of data collection during the interview process, a necessary component for success was the researcher's rapport with the interview participants (Berg, 1989; Glesne & Peshkin, 1992; Mickahail, 2010). When participants felt comfortable, appreciated, and relaxed, they were better able to relate their stories to the interviewer. The Mickahail (2010) study adhered to the guidelines set forth by Fraenkel and Wallen (1993) to establish rapport with the study participants. Open-ended interviews were implemented from those developed around the framework of the research project. This type of questioning allowed each participant to answer the same set of questions but much more freely without restriction on what they answered because they were open-ended. The capturing of their answers in this manner increased the ability to conduct accurate response comparison from a variety of perspectives. Analysis of the data was more easily organized and interviewer bias was reduced by following these guidelines. The significance of the experiences of affected parents and families was related through the oral history interviews and research approach.

> **Research tip:** This study was conducted without the benefit of thematic collection software. For more ease in data analysis, it is highly recommended that researchers utilize the latest version of coding software on the market.

Creating a Poetic Representation of Data

The participants' lived experiences or interviews were studied, analyzed, and presented in poetic display created by Mickahail's distinctive *enlightened pen*. One might ask why she used poetry. In Old Norse tradition, the *skald*, or poet, had a unique societal role to fulfill—a concept related to the social-action focus of the Mickahail (2010) study. Hillman (1999) wrote, "The poet's task is to bring the community to its senses and wake it up" (p. 62). The use of poetic representation in this research also captures the Old Norse skald's spirit of raising the collective community consciousness.

In the Mickahail (2010) research, the *public form* (Eisner 1998), for the data (or transcribed pages of participants' stories from each of the five interviews), were translated into poetic display. The data were displayed aesthetically through a poetic representation format; the *enlightened pen*. Educational criticism and connoisseurship is a qualitative research method that emphasizes the perception of qualities, the interpretation of significance, and the giving of public form to the content of consciousness (Eisner, 1998).

Educational Criticism and Connoisseurship

The oral history interviews were conducted using with Eisner's (1998) dimensions of educational criticism: description, interpretation, evaluation, and thematic analysis. Description is the participant's expressive language, or heart story, which emerged from several structured research interviews. Instead of Eisner's (1998) usual description and collection of data for research through observation, the description and collection of data for this study were conducted through in-depth interviews, using established oral history guidelines (Ritchie, 2010; University of California Berkeley, 2005; Yow, 1994). Eisner (1998) wrote,

> The presence of voice and the use of expressive language are also important in furthering human

> understanding . . . It is called 'empathy.' Why take the heart out of the situations we are trying to help readers understand? (pp. 36-37)

> The participants' voices are validated and recognized through the display, study and analysis of their lived experiences.

Interpretation addresses matters of meaning for the data collected and described (Eisner, 1998). The utilization of the PDAI model allows the interpretation to account for the literal meaning from the recorded interviews. Interpretation is integral to the analysis process, through which Mickahail (2010), as the researcher of the study, a connoisseur of social praxis, disability history, autism, and advocacy, penetrated the essence of participants' heart stories through the poetic display from her *enlightened pen.*

Evaluation intends to assess participants' experiences as change agents in their schools and communities. Portelli (1997) explained that narrators are participants who recall through their memories, a larger perspective of their lived history by highlighting their own anecdotes as participants in the event of interest to the researcher. Thoughtfully developed interview focus questions may also guide the participant into alternative perspectives of their experiences (Sitzia,2003).

Thematic analysis involves "identifying the recurring messages that pervade the situation. A theme is like a pervasive quality [that] . . . permeates and unifies situations" (Eisner, 1998, p. 104). As both a critic (as discloser, not scrutinizer) and connoisseur of the research topic, Mickahail (2010) delved into the experiences of the five participants and provided some evident generalizations or themes, which have practical application to the further change and implementation within educational, medical, parental, and disability communities. Grele (1985) wrote about interviews as a way for participants to "make sense of their lives" (p. viii) at different junctures and turns, while providing novel experience for all to observe. Subsequently, oral history revealed patterns and choices that enabled the interviewer to process their stories

The researcher's role in Eisner's (1998) method is that of a critic and appreciator of the visual arts with an *enlightened eye*. By utilizing the approach of poetic representation to display the analyzed data (Glesne, 1997; Miles & Huberman, 1994 as cited in Mears, 2005; Richardson, 1992, 2002), the Mickahail (2010) study assumed the role of literary critic with the use of an *enlightened pen*. The researcher, with the *enlightened pen* and perceptive appreciation for participants' stories, created aesthetic poetic representations for visual presentation of the interviews.

Research tip: With the growing creative options provided through development in recent technology, a researcher may choose to display data through the creation of word clouds or Wordles. A word cloud (as shown in Figure 2) was created by Wordle Word Cloud (2012) from some of the study's findings. Each poem was written for the purposes of historic preservation of the intent of the narrative interview, yet each poem is also treated as data for analysis. The original "free verse" poetic representation goes beyond the more traditional qualitative interview, expanding the simple narrative's typical boundaries of prose. Poetic representative composition, by expressing the fullness of each individual's story, preserves the vivid "living color" of the storyteller's experience.

Figure 2: Example of Word cloud using findings from Mickahail (2010).

Where to Go From Here?

Reason (1988) articulated the use of interpretative research processes, such as poetic representation, while urging researchers to trust their own intuitive interpretation of their data. Mickahail's (2010) goal was to be congruent with the expressive and research agenda set forth by Eisner (1981) and Finley and Knowles (1995). In many aspects, the poems are understood in much the same way as the qualitative interview from which they were derived, as an exploration of the lived experience of the research participant. This process is affirmed by the aesthetic-educational, qualitative, and oral researchers (Eisner, 1998; Glesne & Peshkin, 1998; Portelli, 1997).

Until the early 1990s, data re-presentation was often separated from research projects (Richardson, 1992). Richardson (1992) viewed data re-presentation as an integral method to the research process rather than apart from the process. By using experimentation with the data in poetic forms, Mickahail (2010) showed the ability in the PDAI model to stimulate experimentation and attention to strategies of data representation with possibilities other than just poetic representations. Poetic representations are as important as prose in representing social research knowledge (Richardson, 2002).

Each poetic representation in the Mickahail (2010) study is the *salafah* of the individual. The salafah is a pre-Islamic narrative genre used by the inhabitants of the Arabian Peninsula to carry the oral history of important past events (Sowayan, 1992). Each poetic narrative or representation in this research is an individual salafah to herald the teller's unique experience of living the history of the organization, FEAT.

To examine visually the poetic representations in the Mickahail (2010) study, one may perceive them flowing as cascading streams. These representations drip with intricacies and meander like persistent waterways, changing the landscape as they flow forward. When contemplating the meaning of the Mickahail study, the individual water paths of poetry meet to forge a waterfall of surging ideas and symbiotic energy. The flow of words may appear to be forcing, pushing and molding change, and powering forth into rapidly expanding moving waters. Examples of the culminating poetry gleaned from the combined five interviews that summarized the data themes and findings, are in this excerpt from the results chapter of the Mickahail study.

We never went
 in the wrong direction.
 We always stayed
 with the empirically based,
 research evidence-based
 practices.
 We got results.
And it was the kid's response
 to treatment --
 that sold the whole thing!

People were coming
 into FEAT
 as they were needed.
 I kept saying,
 "Someone is putting together this puzzle,
 and it's amazing
 that everyone
 keeps coming in
 and coming together......
Now looking back,
 It's not me,
 it's not another parent,
 it's not the doctor,
 but it's letting God
 use us
 to put this puzzle
 together
 so we can help
 those with autism.

Founding FEAT member and research participant, Linda Mayhew, was often the bold person speaking publicly to the media for FEAT in the first two to three years. However, Mayhew's own commentary of her contributions appeared modest. The initial interview with her was followed by two other phone interviews and emails. Her excitement about her work with FEAT and her daughter's development is evident in this single slice from her story.

FEAT-- It's alive.
        It's a heart.
           I keep going back
                to the dinner committee.
        I keep telling them,
           "Don't take the heart out of the night."
The organization is a heart-
        it's the feeling,
           it's the loving,
                it's the caring.
    If you make it about raising more money
              and using your time
        to get the money
              out of people's pockets—
                you lose!
Nancy and I were speaking about this-
        I said,
           "You have to talk to the
committee
        tell them to keep
           the heart
             in the work.
Keep it focused

on the kids!
Keep your speeches
about the children
and what's been happening
for the year.
Remember
the heart -
that's what made FEAT.
That's the
most important
part
of FEAT.
They talk about organizations
being run
like a finely tuned machine,
but that's
not FEAT.
FEAT is
a heart.
FEAT is
people
who really,
really care.
That's why they're there.
It's my definition
of a heart----
people
who care!

Research tip: To avoid difficulties in the data collection and analysis process, researchers may want to study the merits of voice to print software, Dragon Speak or similar voice output software or digitally record the interviews and use qualitative coding software that can automatically take recorded data and transfer the data to text files.

Data Accuracy

How was the data, the interview information, turned into poetic presentation been ensured as accurate with validity and verification? The member verification process accomplished the accuracy check and validity of the qualitative analysis. Member verification of analysis is known to render the conclusions as reliable and verifiable by ensuring the accuracy of the information as true (Janesick, 2010). In the Mickahail (2010) study, participants evaluated the poetic data display of their interview data, and given the opportunity to confirm whether or not the information conveyed their intended answers. In all cases, the information was confirmed. This procedure gave the researcher the green light to proceed with further data analysis. Because the Mickahail study focused on the lived experiences of interview participants, the adherence to ethical standards was essential. Every effort was made to ensure the participants' safety from harm. Each participant was asked to sign a consent form to participate in the study and each enthusiastically agreed to disclose personal identity.

Determining Resultant Themes

Upon completion of the interviews, the transcripts were studied intensively. Essential fragments of the interviews were brought forth and used to create a poetic representation of the interviews. Accuracy was ensured through the validation of the draft version of the poetic data, through a member checking interview session.

The resulting poetic display became the data for final analysis for themes, insights, possible findings, and relevance. A hand-coding method of finding the consistent themes across the interviews was utilized. Being able to capture the essence of the participant stories was accomplished through following the PDAI model as the researcher's guide to vital research.

The Mickahail (2010) study highlighted the themes of the data analysis; direction for advocacy, building for change, and impact of legacy in implementing change in policy at a national and local level. Each theme was distilled into a final poem highlighting the essence of the parent founder's efforts. Each member's contribution can be viewed as a small stream, yet the contributions combine into a grand waterfall. The flowing cascade provides a view of how schools and communities, and ultimately supports children with autism were affected in their reach for their full potential. Through its legacy, FEAT became a surging force, plunging, and furrowing into a rapid river of change that flows throughout the land and beyond.

> **Research tip:** For ease with thematic data analysis, be sure to weigh the merits of data analysis by hand using color coding versus new software on the market.

Findings and Implications of the Approach

The analysis of the founders' lived experiences was presented to answer this researcher's main research questions. Given are the fractal pieces to each person's perspective. As with one picture, the combination of the fractal pieces change a dynamic mural outlining the risks, rewards, community, and wisdom of the FEAT founders. Metaphors for the change-making group emerged from the interviews. Several   interview participants viewed FEAT as a living breathing heart that needs all its members for proper functioning. Others reported FEAT as an evolving organism, extending arms to meet the greater needs of the autism community.

Understanding the Founding of FEAT

This research has focused throughout on the overarching question, "What has been the experience of parents of children with autism who are also founders of the parent organization, FEAT?" This primary research question was explored through the following four sub-questions based on Kotter's Change Model (1996):

1. How did they establish the dynamic advocacy organization FEAT?

2. How do they create change? When successful, what factors contributed to success?

3. What is the importance of their experience? What were their challenges? Their triumphs?

4. Of what benefit would the FEAT experience be to other parent advocacy groups? What advice do they give other parents of children with disabilities?

Of all the findings, the most compelling results were obtained from Question 4.

Autism is increasingly being reported and many are concerned by the nearly epidemic rise in numbers. A recent report of the Centers for Disease Control (CDC) cited autism is occurring in 1 in every 110 school children (CDC, 2009). The 2013 statistic is now 1 in 50 children (Blumberg et al., 2013). Who is more impacted by this crisis than the parents of children with autism? Consistently the numbers or families of children who have autism and seeking high quality services and supports in their schools and communities are growing. As the numbers climb and state and school budgets decline, the need for effective parent advocacy groups, such as FEAT, is paramount. The founders were asked during their interviews what advice would they offer to other groups wanting to advocate for their children, and affect their schools and communities. The founders each had opportunities and time to reflect upon what worked and did not work for their group and its impact. They were precise and thoughtful in articulating their recommendations to parents and others wishing to forge a pioneer change-maker trail, for and those who specifically need early therapy and related services. All of the recommendation lists have implications for anyone who works with children and adults who have autism. This not only includes parents but leaders and laypeople in the education and medical fields and community workers at large. The word cloud (see Figure 2) below was created summarizing the advice the study participants offered to advocating parents and groups seeking change in their schools and communities.

The concluding question after reviewing the process used by Mickahail (2010) built around the PDAI model remains, "How can this model be utilized in another type of specific change process?" Each researcher adapts certain attributes of the Mickahail project while maintaining the use of the PDAI model. The essential components of the PDAI model remain intact with the individual researcher using his or her own choices from each stage. Examples of choices are shown in Figure 3 around each stage of the PDAI model.

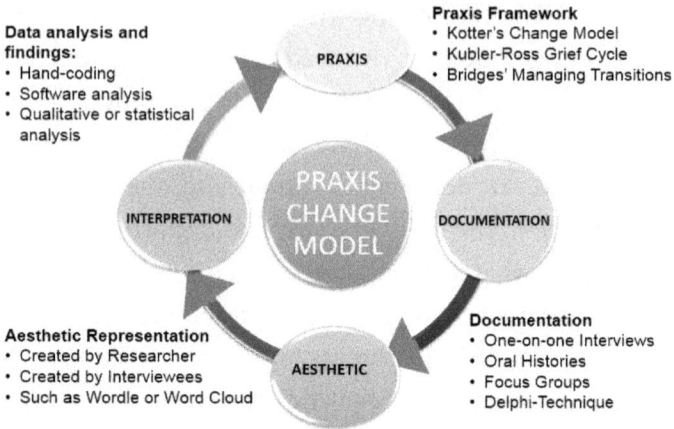

Figure 3. Depicted within this figure are examples of possibilities that may be the outcome of each stage of the PDAI model.

Another function of the PDAI model as a format for the qualitative portion of a mixed-methods design project. Using the PDAI model as the framework for the qualitative portion of a mixed-methods study would achieve a varying method of obtaining and analyzing qualitative narrative oral history. The analysis was derived from the choice of using the PDAI model for the praxis interview questions, the transcribed interview data, and creation of the poetic representation. In a mixed-method project, the resultant themes could be evaluated with a quantitative approach such as surveys, numerical modeling, and quasi-experiments, in order to prioritize, challenge, and substantiate the themes.

Conclusion

By recording and reconstructing FEAT founders' recollections and their roles as change agents for the rights of their children with autism in schools and community, the findings contributed to the greater body of knowledge of the history of disability rights and autism. The Mickahail (2010) research results highlight the role of parent advocacy, and parents' subsequent contributions to shaping foundational legislation, research, and programs in schools and communities. In addition, the research results offer practical insights for equally concerned parent, community and policy making groups as well as the demonstration of the usefulness of a creative, hybrid, and aesthetic research model.

The PDAI model, when employed, requires a researcher to have passionate energy and enthusiasm for novel and significant research using a newly developed hybrid research model. The use of the PDAI model may open previously closed doors for the reader, researcher, and praxis connoisseur, policy planner, implementer, and activist.

References

Anaf J., Baum F., Newman L., Ziersch A., & Jolley G. (2013). The interplay between structure and agency in shaping the mental health consequences of job loss. *BMC Public Health* [serial online], *13*(1), 1-12. Retrieved from http://www.biomedcentral.com/1471-2458/13/110

Arendt, H. (1958). *The human condition.* Chicago, IL: University of Chicago Press.

Autism National Committee. (2009). *Autism facts.* Retrieved from http://www.autcom.org

Blumberg S. J., Bramlett, M. D., Kogan, M. D. , Schieve, L. A., Jones, J. R., & Lu, M. C. (2013). Changes in prevalence of parent-reported autism spectrum disorder in school-aged U.S. children: 2007 to 2011-2012. National Health statistics reports; no 65. Hyattsville, MD: National Center for Health Statistics. Retrieved from http://www.cdc.gov/nchs/data/nhsr/nhsr065.pdf

Berg, B. L. (1989). *Qualitative research methods for the social sciences.* Los Angeles, CA: Allyn & Bacon.

Bridges, W. (2009). *Managing transitions: Making the most of change* (3rd ed.). Philadelphia, PA: Perseus Books Group.

Centers for Disease Control and Prevention (CDC). (2009). Prevalence of autism spectrum disorders – autism and developmental disabilities monitoring network, United States, 2006. *Morbidity and Mortality Weekly Report Surveillance Summaries 2006.* Retrieved from http://www.cdc.gov/mmwr/preview/mmwrhtml/ss5810a1.htm

Denzin, N. (1970). *The research act in sociology: A theoretical introduction to sociological methods.* Chicago, IL: Aldine.

Eisner, E. W. (1981). On the differences between scientific and artistic approaches to qualitative research. *Educational Researcher, 10*(4), 5-9. doi:10.3102/0013189X010004005

Eisner, E. W. (1998). *The enlightened eye: Qualitative research and the enhancement of educational practice.* Upper Saddle River, NJ: Merrill.

Families for the Early Autism Treatment. (FEAT). (2009, August 23). *Families for early autism treatment.* Retrieved from http://www.feat.org

Finley, S., & Knowles, J. G. (1995). Researcher as artist/artist as researcher.

Qualitative Inquiry, 1(1), 110-142. doi:10.1177/107780049500100107

Fraenkel, J., & Wallen, N. E. (1993). *How to design and evaluate research in education*. New York, NY: McGraw-Hill.

Frisch, M. (1990). Quality in history programs. In *A shared authority: Essays on the craft and meaning of oral and public history*. Albany, NY: New York State University.

Glesne, C. (1997). That rare feeling: Re-presenting research through poetic transcription, *Qualitative Inquiry, 3*(2), 202-222.

Glesne, C., & Peshkin, A. (1992). *Becoming qualitative researchers: An introduction*. White Plains, NY: Longman.

Grele, R. J. (1985). Movement without aim: Methodological and theoretical problems in oral history. In R. J. Grele (Ed.), *Envelopes of sound: The art of oral history* (2nd ed.). Chicago, IL: Precedent.

Janesick, V. J. (2010). *Oral history for the qualitative researcher: Choreographing the story*. New York, NY: The Guilford.

Hillman, J. (1999). *The force of character and the lasting life*. New York, NY: Random House.

Kotter, J. P. (1996). *Leading change*. Boston, MA: Harvard Business School. Retrieved from http://drbethany.files.wordpress.com/2013/04/kotter-interview-model.pdf

Kotter, J. P. (2006). *Our iceberg is melting*. New York, NY: St. Martin's. Retrieved from http://drbethany.wordpress.com/2013/04/14/kotters-stage-change-model-as-iceberg/

Kotter, J. P. (2008). *A sense of urgency*. Boston, MA: Harvard Business School.

Mears, C. (2005). *Experiences of Columbine parents: Finding a way back to tomorrow* (Doctoral dissertation). Denver University College of Education.

Mickahail, B. K. (2010). *Parents as change agents in their schools and communities* (Doctoral dissertation). Denver University, Morgridge College of Education.

Miles, M., & Huberman, A. M. (1994). *Qualitative data analysis* (2nd ed.). Thousand Oaks, CA: Sage.

Portelli, A. (1997). *The battle of Valle Guile: Oral history and the art of dialogue*. Madison, WI: The University of Wisconsin.

Reason, P. (1988). *Human inquiry in action: Developments in new paradigm research*. London, UK: Sage.

Richardson, L. (1992). The consequences of poetic representation. In C. Ellis & M. G. Lathery (Eds.), *Investigating subjectivity: Research on lived experience* (pp. 125-137). Thousand Oaks, CA: Sage.

Richardson, L. (2002). Poetic representations of interviews. In J. F. Gubrium, & J. A. Holstein (Eds.), *Handbook of interview research: Context and method* (pp. 877-891). Thousand Oaks, CA: Sage

Ritchie, D. A. (2010). *The Oxford handbook of oral history*. Oxford University.

Seidman, I. (2006). *Interviewing as qualitative research: A guide for researchers in education and the social sciences* (3rd ed.). New York, NY: Teacher's College.

Sitzia, L. (2003). A shared authority: An impossible goal? *The Oral History Review, 30*(1), 87-101.

Sowayan, S. A. (1992). *The Arabian oral historical narrative: An ethnographic and linguistic analysis*. Wiesbaden, Germany: Otto Harrassowitz.

Thompson, P. (2000). *The voice of the past: Oral history* (3rd ed.). New York, NY: Oxford University.

University of California Berkley. (2004). *Oral history of disability rights project: Gunnar Dybwad, pioneer in the parents' movement: The campaign for public office*. Berkeley, CA: The Bancroft Library, University of California. Retrieved from http://bancroft.berkeley.edu/collections/drilm/collection/items/dybwad.html

Wordle Word Cloud. (2012). *Wordle word cloud*. Retrieved from http://www.wordlewordcloud.com/

Yow, R. V. (1994). *Recording oral history: A practical guide for social scientists*. Thousand Oaks, CA: Sage.

About the Author...

Dr. Bethany Mickahail resides in California. Dr. Bethany holds a Bachelor of Arts, in Linguistics & TESL from the University of Hawaii at Manoa: a Masters of International Affairs and Communications from the School of International & Public Affairs at Columbia University, NYC; and a Doctorate in Educational Leadership & Public Policy from the University of Denver.

Dr. Bethany has provided over 20 years of learning opportunities to children and adults as an ESL teacher, staff developer-trainer, district wide program coordinator, college educator and United Nations researcher. Dr. Bethany's recent efforts focus on innovative community based disability program policy, development, training and systems change in California. Her current research pursuits include societal praxis and innovation.

She frequently speaks to groups about disability policy development and implementation. She served as a member of a state legislative subcommittee. Her dissertation titled, *Parents as Change Agents in their Schools and Communities,* inspires parent and policy-making groups to be relentless in their advocacy for high quality lifelong services for people with disabilities.

As global traveler, societal praxis poet-pioneer, and cultural connoisseur, Dr. Bethany enjoys singing, exploring art, water, and nature with her wonderful husband and two children.

To reach Dr. Bethany Mickahail for consulting or dissertation coaching, please e-mail: bmickahail@comcast.net

To contact Dr. Mickahail' nonprofit organization, visit http://scholarshiplighthouse.com/

About the Author...

Ph.D. Psychology, U.S. International University; MA Psychology, U.S. International University; MA Education, American Intercontinental University; BS Mathematics, San Diego State University; Editor of two European and one American journal; Published author in many peer-reviewed journals, past chairperson of California Psychological Association, Division 3.

Her experience at the university level includes instructing statistics and research, psychology courses in family systems, drug addiction, counseling, communication, motivation, and leadership. In Romania, Dr. Andrews created a course entitled "Faith-based Psychology and Counseling."

After receiving her MA, Dr. Andrews worked with pregnant addicts providing a complete life program. She transitioned to coaching executives, teams, and employees. She developed numerous courses for leadership and conducted training in life situations including parenting and communication strategies for employees.

Dr. Kate spent 2 years in Israel working and lived in Romania for 8 years working with teenage orphans through a non-profit organization she directs. Between research, teaching, and writing, she currently finds time for her five, soon-to-be six grandchildren.

She has five current research projects in action, edits dissertations for APA, and provides methodology guidance for doctoral students. For dissertation coaching or speaking engagements, Dr. Andrews may be contacted at kandrews64@ yahoo.com

To contact Dr. Andrews' nonprofit organization, visit http://scholarshiplighthouse.com/

CHAPTER 8

Using Phenomenological Design to Explore Knowledge Sharing

By Dr. Melissa A. Connell & Dr. Judith Fisher-Blando

Leaders, managers, and employees do not completely understand the knowledge sharing process between individuals and within the social structure of teams (Blankenship & Ruona, 2009; Kokavcova & Mala, 2009). An average-sized company with 1,000 employees could incur approximately $6 million in productivity costs when obtainable knowledge within an organization is not shared (Keyes, 2008). Organizations that do not implement knowledge management strategies will not remain competitive in the 21st century (Gregory-Mina, 2010). The purpose of Connell's (2013) qualitative, phenomenological research study was to acquire new knowledge by exploring the lived experiences of employees within the contracting division at a federal organization and to provide management with a better understanding of the knowledge sharing process. As part of this phenomenological research study, Connell used Nonaka and Takeuchi's socialization, externalization, internalization, and combination model to explore the organized, continual method of tacit-to-explicit knowledge theory for organizational knowledge creation. The intent of this chapter is to provide readers and refractive thinkers with a better understanding of the qualitative, phenomenological research design process while exploring knowledge sharing and leadership styles businesses are using to share and manage knowledge in the 21st century.

Knowledge Sharing

Knowledge refers to information combined with expertise, circumstance, understanding, and thought (Bennet & Bennet, 2008). Knowledge consists of several types, including implicit, explicit, tacit, or a combination (Bennet & Bennet, 2008). These attributes, when combined, are a high-value form of information, which supports decisions and actions. A significant aspect of knowledge management is knowledge sharing; however, leaders, managers, and employees do not completely understand the knowledge sharing process between individuals and within the social structure of teams (Blankenship & Ruona, 2009; Kokavcova & Mala, 2009). The concept of knowledge dates back to the ancient period, 551 to 300 before the common era, by Western philosophers to include Aristotle, Plato, and Socrates and Eastern philosophers such as Confucius with the thought process of wanting to know (Wiig, 1997). During the 1950s, theories emerged about whether organizations could enhance the learning process to make businesses more efficient (Edwards et al., 2009). By the late 20th century, many businesses were implementing Total Quality Management (TQM) and focusing on the cognitive sciences with the intent of improving effectiveness in the workplace (Wiig, 1997). Alolayyan, Ali, and Idris (2011) defined TQM as integrated organizational practices used to implement quality measurements and continuous process improvements of procedures, products, and services to exceed customer expectations.

Between the late 20th and early 21st centuries, knowledge management practices focused predominantly on acquiring explicit knowledge, consisting of documented knowledge (Gonzaga, 2009). In the 21st century, the need to manage knowledge is more critical than ever because of the increased number of experienced employees retiring within the next 3 to 5 years (Appelbaum et al., 2012; Martins & Meyer, 2012). Other researchers found that the traditional, one-on-one style of mentoring is not the preferred method for Generation X (Gen X) and Generation Y (Gen Y) workers (McNichols, 2010). In the 21st century, management scholars and business professionals are still searching for ways to manage knowledge but cannot come up with an accepted process by the general business community (Wiig, 1997). With businesses in the 21st century facing the challenges of a changing workforce, the need for organizations to share and manage knowledge is necessary to improve efficiency and increase competitive advantage (Lin & Chen, 2008). Leadership approaches that businesses perceive as important to share and manage knowledge in the 21st century are transformational and transactional leadership styles (Trottier, Van Wart, & Wang, 2008).

Transformational Leadership
Transformational leaders inspire and empower their employees to surpass goals and to achieve more than originally expected. Transformational leaders place organizational interests before self-interests and transform their employees into leaders (Bass, 2003). Transformational leaders empower employees through their own actions and behaviors, which as a result motivates employees to identify with and emulate the leader (Avey, Hughes, Norman, & Luthans, 2008; Bass, 2003). The skill-set consistent with transformational leadership and refractive thinking promotes employees' intellectual stimulation and expansion of their own

abilities and thought-processes (Avey et al., 2008; Bass, 2003). Because different generations—Baby Boomers, Gen X, and Gen Y— offer different methods of thinking and working together on a day-to-day basis, leaders need to understand and implement transformational leadership to guide and direct their employees (Green & Roberts, 2012); Zopiatis & Constanti, 2012).

Transformational leadership involves several bases, including (a) individuals having a strong personal relationship with the leader, (b) a common vision for the organization's future, and (c) employees working together as a team for the advancement of the organization (Schneider & George, 2011). The transformational leader is charismatic, motivational, inspirational, goal-oriented, confident, a visionary, and one who attracts followers, or workers, through personal, individual relationships (Schneider & George, 2011). De Vries, Bakker-Pieper, and Oostenveld (2010) described the charismatic leader as compassionate and meticulous, with a nonthreatening style of communication. Transformational leaders encourage and stimulate workers to exceed expectations within their job responsibilities and have an approach to work that encourages a team-based environment in addition to providing individualized consideration that facilitates learning, promotes trust, and supports innovative ideas from employees (Gregory, Moates, & Gregory, 2011). Businesses in the 21st century may need to focus their attention on and recruit leaders who possess transformational characteristics, which complement and enhance the knowledge sharing process.

A correlation exists between transformational leadership and innovation (Paulsen, Maldonado, Callan, & Ayoko, 2009). The transformational leader supports the team through the promotion of new thoughts and ideas, which leads to improvements and innovation. Lee, Gillespie, Mann, and Wearing (2010) added a relationship exists between transformational leadership and trust. Transformational leadership is the most resilient and most effective form of leadership during organizational change (Herold, Fedor, Caldwell, & Liu, 2008). Transformational leadership is resistant during organizational change because leaders have formed personal relationships with the individuals they supervise (Graham, 2008). However, with new challenges facing businesses of the 21st century, such as generational differences within the workforce, organizational leaders must maintain a sense of openness and willingness to change and maintain flexibility or face the consequences of personnel and talent shortages (Green & Roberts, 2012).

Kayemuddin (2012) suggested that effective leaders have the ability to inspire, motivate, and encourage individuals to overcome obstacles by fulfilling essential needs, while achieving designated tasks that contribute to the organization's mission. Zopiatis and Constanti (2012) concluded that several attributes of the transformational leader consist of being extroverted, conscientious, agreeable, open, considerate, and knowledgeable, with the result having a direct influence on employee motivation and performance. Because of these characteristics, researchers have indicated that leaders who possess transformational-type behaviors are more likely to achieve the best performance from individuals (Zopiatis & Constanti, 2012).

Transformational leaders project their attention away from a self-seeking style of leadership to a self-sacrificing approach, focusing on other individuals and team members within their organization (Simola, Barling, & Turner, 2012). Sarros and Santora (2001) concluded that leaders who display characteristics such as self-perception, motivation, and empathy appear to be more valuable to the organization than those without these attributes. Transformational leaders are thought of by many scholars as the most competent for managing businesses in the 21st century.

Transactional Leadership

The second leadership model, which received differing views in the knowledge management community, is transactional leadership. Sarros and Santora (2001) posited that the basis for transactional leadership consists of meeting employees' physical and mental needs in return for projected work performance. Analoui, Doloriert, and Sambrook (2013), Behery (2008), and Sarros and Santora (2001) further theorized that transactional leadership consists of two parts, including contingent reward and management by exception.

The outcome for leaders using contingent reward is achieving results (Sarros & Santora, 2001). In addition, contingent reward consists of a mutual relationship between managers, leaders, and employees who exchange knowledge, ideas, and skills with the purpose of fulfilling organizational goals and individual wants and needs (Analoui et al., 2013; Behery, 2008; Sarros & Santora, 2001). Analoui et al. (2013) and Behery (2008) further summarized that contingent reward occurs when the negotiated agreement between the manager and the employee results in positive efforts, satisfactory performance, and recognized accomplishments. Sarros and Santora (2001) further emphasized a negative aspect of using contingent reward is leaders visualizing performance in terms of money for the organization, easily forgetting the needs and wants of individual workers, and the mutual agreement that exists between leaders and workers to achieve desired outcomes.

When practicing management by exception, leaders anticipate employees completing assignments to an adequate standard (Sarros & Santora, 2001). Sarros and Santora (2001) concluded that transactional leaders do not motivate, encourage, or stimulate employees to achieve beyond the required results. Behery (2008) further defined management by exception as divided into two parts, active and passive. Active management by exception involves monitoring employee behavior and taking corrective action when appropriate, to ensure work meets satisfactory standards (Analoui et al., 2012; Behery, 2008). Passive management by exception occurs when the employee fails to meet the agreed upon standards (Behery, 2008). Leaders practicing management by exception foresee little advantage to new perspectives or strategies (Sarros & Santora, 2001). Instead, if the goal is achieved, workers are pleased, and the business continues to exist, management by exception served its purpose of achieving targeted results (Sarros & Santora, 2001).

Qualitative Method Used

Qualitative, phenomenological research was the method used, which enabled the researcher to observe personally the knowledge and skills between the two groups of government contracting professionals. Qualitative research was the preferred method of study to analyze the issues, claims, and concerns behind the employees' experiences regarding knowledge sharing between the experienced and the new or inexperienced employees within the contracting division at a federal organization. The qualitative study also explored the employees' lived experiences to provide management with a better understanding of the knowledge sharing process. Worasinchai, Ribiere, and Arntzen (2008) used qualitative research to determine the overall structure for cultivating research alliances and knowledge transfer between universities and industries in Thailand. Likewise, Burns, Acar, and Datta (2011) found that qualitative research was a beneficial approach to examine knowledge sharing as it relates to consumer product development. Tong and Mitra (2009) argued that qualitative research was the best way to address how culture influences knowledge management practices within Chinese industries. Therefore, using a qualitative research approach to determine the issues, claims, and concerns behind the employees' perceptions regarding knowledge sharing was appropriate. Madill and Gough (2009) concluded that qualitative research is a method of observing, investigating, and comprehending a particular problem or issue associated with an individual or within a social group. The use of qualitative research allows the ability to ask open-ended, fact-finding questions, and collect data within the participant's surroundings, with the intent of moving from a specific to broad-spectrum of ideas with collective data (Madill & Gough, 2009).

Qualitative research is an inductive approach where participants' personal experiences, when recorded during the interview and compiled together, become the results of the study (Gelo, Braakmann, & Benetka, 2008). Gelo et al. (2008) further concluded that the intent of qualitative research is to develop an acceptable theory derived from the observations made. Eriksson and Kovalainen (2008) further concluded that qualitative research is especially pertinent and applicable when previous knowledge about an existing problem is modest or limited. Qualitative research tends to be a probing, adaptable, and adjustable type of investigative study that focuses on unstructured problems (Eriksson & Kovalainen, 2008). Pratt (2009) concluded that qualitative research starts with questions, with the ultimate purpose of gaining knowledge and learning about the aspects of the social world. Moreover, qualitative research is an appropriate approach to gather information relating to *how* questions as opposed to *how many*, for understanding the lived experiences of the participants interviewed (Pratt, 2009).

Qualitative research was the preferred method to analyze the issues, claims, and concerns behind the employees' perceptions regarding knowledge sharing between the experienced and the new or inexperienced employees. The study also provided management with a better understanding of the knowledge sharing process. Prior to selecting qualitative research as the preferred method of study, a comparison between methodologies determined the most advantageous method for Connell's (2013) research. Qualitative research concentrates on investigating, examining, and understanding information; whereas, quantitative research focuses on justifying, testing of assumptions, and statistical analysis (Eriksson & Kovalainen, 2008). Qualitative research concentrates on a holistic understanding of the problem studied; whereas, quantitative research centers on organized, consistent, and the theoretical approach of collecting and analyzing experimental data. Quantitative research does not have the capability to deal with the social and cultural aspects of the problem (Eriksson & Kovalainen, 2008).

Eriksson and Kovalainen (2008), along with McGrath and O'Toole (2012), suggested that the researcher's worldview, created through a particular culture and various experiences, often affects the specific research methodology. Tacit knowledge is unwritten knowledge that begins in the mind of an individual, conveyed in the form of learning by acting and by learning vicariously, which can be difficult to verbalize (Ngah & Jusoff, 2009). Explicit knowledge consists of written knowledge gathered in a particular form, easily shared and openly available (DeHaven, 2007). Because knowledge, specifically tacit knowledge, exists with the individual worker, the qualitative, phenomenological design was the most appropriate type of research to probe the minds of the participants to understand the problem.

Phenomenological Design

With the use of qualitative research, specifically the phenomenological approach, the observation of the personal experiences of a select group of participants occurred to understand patterns or behaviors (Cassidy et al., 2011). Fowlie and Wood (2009) used the phenomenological approach to determine which emotionally intelligent proficiencies have more of an impact during times of change. Likewise, Searle and Hanrahan (2011) found that the phenomenological approach was a beneficial approach to understand the leadership characteristics that motivate and inspire others. Savage-Austin and Honeycutt (2011) argued that the phenomenological approach was the best way to address how leaders motivate individuals to accomplish organizational goals. Therefore, using the phenomenological approach to determine the employees' perceptions regarding knowledge sharing within the contracting division at a federal organization was suitable.

Qualitative, phenomenological research was the preferred approach, which allowed for the examination, uncovering, and understanding of the employees' views and opinions regarding knowledge sharing. The socialization, externalization, combination, and internalization (SECI) model developed by Nonaka and Takeuchi in 1995 represented an organized, continuous method for the transfer of tacit to explicit knowledge; consequently, sharing new thoughts occurs when the components of mutual trust and a common situation exists (DeHaven, 2007). Phenomenological research uncovers the answers with the use of fact-finding questions to uncover real-world experiences that exist with individuals based on their own perception.

The theory behind the phenomenological approach emphasizes the social characteristics of research, with the premise of flexibility of ideas during the study, which consist of changing assumptions that influence the way of conducting research (Eriksson & Kovalainen, 2008). This theory allows for ongoing adjustments, admission of new ideas, and approval of new items in the creation of the study (Eriksson & Kovalainen, 2008). Because knowledge, specifically tacit knowledge, exists with the individual worker, the phenomenological design was the most appropriate type of research to probe the minds of the participants to understand the problem. The quantitative approach would not have allowed for the use of open-ended questions, only to analyze numbers and collect data (Eriksson & Kovalainen, 2008). Because knowledge, specifically tacit knowledge, exists with the individual worker, the phenomenological design using a semistructured, face-to-face interview approach was the most appropriate type of research to probe the minds of the participants to understand the problem, and seek clarification regarding the phenomena (Ramm & Kane, 2011).

Research Process

Twenty participants, consisting of government-contracting professionals possessing 5 years or less experience and senior employees with 10 years or more experience, shared their lived experiences while responding to 17 interview questions. The central research question addressed the issues, claims, and concerns behind the employees' perceptions regarding knowledge sharing within the contracting division at a federal organization. After interviews were conducted, analyzing data occurred using HyperRESEARCH to identify factors that the participants perceive as important to increase knowledge sharing among government employees. Coding, analyzing, and grouping data into 10 primary themes occurred after conducting the personal, semi-structured interviews. Results indicated that the foundation for supporting the knowledge sharing process consists of implementing a culture of openness and willingness to share from upper management to individual employees and between individual workers.

Applications and Recommendations

The findings of the research study regarding the employees' perceptions of knowledge sharing within the contracting division at a federal organization are important indicators that government contracting organizations should focus on when deliberating over their business strategies. The 20 contracting professionals interviewed consisted of two groups, government-contracting professionals possessing 5 years or less contracting experience and senior contracting professionals with 10 years or more experience. Participants provided consensus that implementing knowledge management principles would benefit and improve business practices within the federal organization as well as other government entities. Implementing knowledge management principles consists of improved attitudes, positive relationships, and increases in job performance. Implementing these same knowledge-sharing processes within other government entities internally and externally to achieve positive knowledge sharing results can improve present business practices within the government and other entities throughout the business community.

Conclusion

We leave it to the researcher to decide if a qualitative phenomenological study is the right method of choice for their topic and cause. The purpose of Connell's (2013) qualitative, phenomenological research study was to analyze and explore the individual perceptions of the experienced and the inexperienced employees within the contracting division at a federal organization and to provide management with a better understanding of the knowledge sharing process. Qualitative research was the preferred method to analyze and explore the individual perceptions of the experienced and the inexperienced employees. As the preferred method, the phenomenological approach focused on identifying the participant's subjective experiences and interpretations of events through a process of interviews and observations. With a concentrated effort given to organizational culture, management support, and leadership, and trust within the organization, areas of concerns such as a lack of motivation, negative attitudes, individual perception, and personality, uncertainty regarding personal relationships, and an increased workload within the organization would cease to be a major obstacle in facilitating and improving knowledge sharing within the organization. With businesses in the 21st century facing the challenges of a changing workforce and generational differences in the workplace, the need for organizations to share and manage knowledge is necessary to become refractive thinkers who not only *think out-of-the-box*, but who have *eliminated* the box.

References

Alolayyan, M. N., Ali, K. A., & Idris, F. (2011). The influence of Total Quality Management (TQM) on operational flexibility in Jordanian hospitals: Medical workers' perspectives. *Asian Journal on Quality*, *12*, 204-222. doi:10.1108/15982681111158751

Analoui, B. D., Doloriert, C. H., & Sambrook, S. (2013). Leadership and knowledge management in UK ICT organisations. *Journal of Management Development*, *32*, 4-17. doi:10.1108/02621711311286892

Appelbaum, S. H., Gunkel, H., Benyo, C., Ramadan, S., Sakkal, F., & Wolff, D. (2012). Transferring corporate knowledge via succession planning: Analysis and solutions–Part 1. *Industrial and Commercial Training*, *44*, 281-289. doi:10.1108/00197851211245031

Avey, J. B., Hughes, L. W., Norman, S. M., & Luthans, K. W. (2008). Using positivity, transformational leadership and empowerment to combat employee negativity. *Leadership & Organization Development Journal*, *29*, 110-126. doi:10.1108/01437730810852470

Bass, B. M. (2003). Face to face - power to change: A conversation with Bernard M. Bass. *Leadership in Action*, *23*, 9-11. doi:10.1002/lia.1013

Behery, M. H. (2008). Leadership, knowledge sharing, and organizational benefits within the UAE. *Journal of American Academy of Business, Cambridge*, *12, 227-236*. Retrieved from http://www.jaabc.com

Bennet, D., & Bennet, A. (2008). Engaging tacit knowledge in support of organizational learning. *VINE: The Journal of Information and Knowledge Management Systems*, *38*, 72-94. doi:10.1108/03055720810870905

Blankenship, S. S., & Ruona, W. E. (2009). Exploring knowledge sharing in social structures: Potential contributions to an overall knowledge management strategy. *Advances in Developing Human Resources*, *11*, 290-306. doi:10.1177/1523422309338578

Cassidy, E., Reynolds, F., Naylor, S., & De Souza, L. (2011). Using interpretative phenomenological analysis to inform physiotherapy practice: An introduction with reference to the lived experience of cerebellar ataxia. *Physiotherapy Theory and Practice*, *27*, 263-277. doi:10.3109/09593985.2010.488278

Connell, M. (2013). *Exploring knowledge sharing in the Department of Defense.* Manuscript submitted for publication.

DeHaven, D. (2007). *The influence of servant leadership on knowledge management: An investigation of certified knowledge manager perceptions* (Doctoral dissertation). Available from ProQuest Dissertations and Theses database. (UMI No. 3274708)

de Vries, R. E., Bakker-Pieper, A., & Oosternveld, W. (2010). Leadership=communication? The relations of leaders' communication styles with leadership styles, knowledge sharing and leadership outcomes. *Journal of Business and Psychology, 25*, 367-380. doi:10.1007/s10869-009-9140-2

Edwards, J. S., Ababneh, B., Hall, M., & Shaw, D. (2009). Knowledge management: A review of the field and of OR's contribution. *Journal of the Operational Research Society, 60*, 114-126. doi:10.1057/jors.2008.168

Eriksson, P., & Kovalainen, A. (2008). *Qualitative methods in business research.* Thousand Oaks, CA: Sage.

Fowlie, J., & Wood, M. (2009). The emotional impact of leaders' behaviours. *Journal of European Industrial Training, 33*, 559-572. doi:10.1108/03090590910974428

Gelo, O., Braakmann, D., & Benetka, G. (2008). Quantitative and qualitative research: Beyond the debate. *Integrative Psychological and Behavioral Science, 42*, 266-290. doi:10.1007/s12124-008-9078-3

Gonzaga, S. (2009). *Exploring knowledge exchange between senior and future leaders: A grounded-theory study* (Doctoral dissertation). Retrieved from ProQuest Dissertations and Theses database. (UMI No. 3405039)

Graham, J. (2008). *Leadership and change in a crisis organization: An exploratory analysis of the relationship between leadership style and employee participation* (Doctoral dissertation). Retrieved from ProQuest Dissertations and Theses database. (UMI No. 3339019)

Green, D. D., & Roberts, G. E. (2012). Impact of postmodernism on public sector leadership practices: Federal government human capital development implications. *Public Personnel Management. 41*(1), 79-96. Retrieved from http://www.ipma-hr.org/publications/ppmlogin

Gregory, B. T., Moates, N., & Gregory S. T. (2011). An exploration of perspective taking as an antecedent of transformational leadership behavior. *Leadership & Organization Development Journal, 32,* 807-816. doi:10.1108/01437731111183748

Gregory-Mina, H. J. (2010, December). The importance of teams and how to lead teams through change initiatives in the 21st century organizations. *The Business Review, Cambridge, 16*(1), 60-66. Retrieved from http://www.jaabc.com

Herold, D. M., Fedor, D. B., Caldwell, S., & Liu, Y. (2008). The effects of transformational and change leadership on employees' commitment to a change: A multi-level study. *Journal of Applied Psychology, 93,* 346-357. doi:10.1037/0021-9010.93.2.346

Kayemuddin, M. D. (2012). Leadership in small business in Bangladesh. *International Journal of Entrepreneurship, 16,* 25-35. Retrieved from http://www.alliedacademies.org

Keyes, J. (2008). *Identifying the barriers to knowledge sharing in knowledge intensive organizations* (Doctoral dissertation). Retrieved from ProQuest Dissertations and Theses database. (UMI No. 3316911)

Kokavcova, D., & Mala, D. (2009). Knowledge sharing - the main prerequisite of innovation. *Organizacijø Vadyba: Sisteminiai Tyrimai, 51*(1), 47-56. Retrieved from *http://www.ceeol.com/*

Lee, P., Gillespie, N., Mann, L., & Wearing, A. (2010). Leadership and trust: Their effect on knowledge sharing and team performance. *Management Learning, 41,* 473-491. doi:10.1177/1350507610362036

Lin, M.-J., & Chen, C.-J. (2008). Integration and knowledge sharing: Transforming to long-term competitive advantage. *International Journal of Organizational Analysis, 16,* 83-84. doi:10.1108/19348830810915514

Madill, A., & Gough, B. (2009). Qualitative research and its place in psychological science. *Psychological Methods, 13,* 254-271. doi:10.1037/a0013220

Martins, E. C., & Meyer, W. J. (2012). Organizational and behavioral factors that influence knowledge retention. *Journal of Knowledge Management, 16,* 77-96. doi:10.1108/13673271211198954

McGrath, H., & O'Toole, T. (2012). Critical issues in research design in action research in an SME development context. *European Journal of Training and Development, 36*, 508-526. doi:10.1108/03090591211232075

McNichols, D. (2010). Optimal knowledge transfer methods: A generation x perspective. *Journal of Knowledge Management, 14*, 24-40. doi:10.1108/13673271011015543

Ngah, R., & Jusoff, K. (2009). Tacit knowledge sharing and SME's organizational performance. *International Journal of Economics and Finance, 1*(1), 216-220. Retrieved from http://www.ccsenet.org/journal/index.php/ijef

Nonaka, I., & Takeuchi, H. (1995). *The knowledge-creating company*. New York, NY: Oxford University Press.

Paulsen, N., Maldonado, D., Callan, V. J., & Ayoko, O. (2009). Charismatic leadership, change and innovation in an R&D organization. *Journal of Organizational Change Management, 22*, 47-55. doi:10.1108/09534810910983479

Pratt, M. G. (2009). For the lack of a boilerplate: Tips on writing up and (and reviewing) qualitative research. *Academy of Management Journal, 52*, 856-862. doi:10.5465/AMJ.2009.44632557

Ramm, D., & Kane, R. (2011). A qualitative study exploring the emotional responses of female patients learning to perform clean intermittent self-catheterisation. *Journal of Clinical Nursing, 20*, 3152-3162. doi:10.1111/j.1365-2702.2011.03779.x

Sarros, J. C., & Santora, J. C. (2001). The transformational-transactional leadership model in practice. *Leadership & Organization Development Journal, 22*, 383-394. doi:10.1108/01437730110410107

Savage-Austin, A. R., & Honeycutt, A. (2011). Servant leadership: A phenomenological study of practices, experiences, organizational effectiveness, and barriers. *Journal of Business & Economics Research, 9*, 49-54. Retrieved from http://www.journals.cluteonline.com/

Schneider, S. K., & George, W. M. (2011). Servant leadership versus transformational leadership in voluntary service organizations. *Leadership & Organization Development Journal, 32*, 60-77. doi:10.1108/01437731111099283

Searle, G. D., & Hanrahan, S. J. (2011). Leading to inspire others: Charismatic influence or hard work? *Leadership & Organization Development Journal, 32*, 736-754. doi:10.1108/01437731111170021

Simola, S., Barling, J., & Turner, N. (2012). Transformational leadership and leaders' mode of care reasoning. *Journal of Business Ethics, 108*, 229-237. doi:10.1007/s10551-011-1080-x

Tong, J., & Mitra, A. (2009). Chinese cultural influences on knowledge management practice. *Journal of Knowledge Management, 13*, 49-62. doi:10.1108/13673270910942691

Trottier, T., Van Wart, M., & Wang, X. (2008). Examining the nature and significance of leadership in government organizations. *Public Administration Review, 68* (2), 319-333. doi: 10.1111/j.1540-6210.2007.00865.x.

Wiig, K. M. (1997). Knowledge management: Where did it come from and where will it go? *Expert Systems with Applications, 13*, 1-14. doi:10.1016/S0957-4174(97)00018-3

Worasinchai, L., Ribiere, V. M., & Arntzen, A. A. (2008). Working knowledge, the university-industry linkage in Thailand: Concepts and issues. *VINE: The Journal of Information and Knowledge Management Systems, 38*, 507-524. doi:10.1108/03055720810917741

Zopiatis, A., & Constanti, P. (2012). Extraversion, openness and conscientiousness: The route to transformational leadership in the hotel industry. *Leadership & Organization Development Journal, 33*, 86-104. doi:10.1108/01437731211193133

About the Author...

Charleston, South Carolina author Dr. Melissa A. Connell holds several accredited degrees to include: a Bachelor of Arts (BA) in Journalism from the University of South Carolina; a Master of Business Administration (MBA) from Charleston Southern University; and a Doctorate of Business Administration (DBA) from Walden University. She has also obtained her Lean Six Sigma Green Belt certification.

Dr. Melissa has over 7 years of experience as a Contract Specialist working with the federal government as well as 21 years of extensive and diverse experience working in non-governmental organizations with knowledge ranging in the areas of human resources, volunteer recruitment and coordination, sales, fundraising, written and verbal communications, and public relations.

She is an expert on Knowledge Sharing, having written her research doctoral study on *Exploring Knowledge Sharing in the Department of Defense.* Her goal is to educate leaders, managers, and employees on knowledge management principles to encourage a more competent, successful, and effective work and business environment.

To reach Dr. Melissa A. Connell for information on knowledge sharing, please e-mail: connell@homesc.com

About the Author...

Southern California author Dr. Judy Fisher-Blando holds several accredited degrees: a Bachelor of Science (BS) in Business Management; a Master's of Art (MA) in Organizational Management; and a Doctorate of Management (DM) in Organizational Leadership from the University of Phoenix School of Advanced Studies. She has also obtained her Six Sigma Black Belt certificate.

Dr. Judy is an adjunct professor for Walden University, Capella University, and University of Phoenix, teaching classes in organizational behavior, ethical responsibility, and research methods. She is an expert on Workplace Bullying, having written her research dissertation on *Workplace Bullying: Aggressive Behavior and Its Effect on Job Satisfaction and Productivity.* In addition, she is a Life Coach, coaching leaders on how to develop High Performance Organizations, coaching the targets of workplace bullies, and giving presentations on Finding and Measuring your Joy.

To reach Dr. Judy Fisher-Blando for information on any of these topics, and for executive coaching or coaching for workplace bullying, please e-mail judyblando@gmail.com

CHAPTER 9

Transformative Learning Through the Lens of
Transcendental Phenomenology: A Study Design Overview

By Dan Santangelo, Ed.D.

This chapter includes a step-by-step examination of how a transcendental phenomenological study design is applied to the exploration of a lived experience. This examination provides an overview of some of the primary differences among three distinct phenomenological approaches and how to recognize and apply these approaches in a research-based setting.   An exploration of the appropriateness of the transcendental phenomenological study design combined with a precise definition of validity and reliability provides the learner with a model for developing the dissertation proposal.   Data collection, instrumentation, and data analysis commonly used under the transcendental phenomenological rubric is thoughtfully examined using a concise and engaging format.

This chapter also incorporates an examination of the research design applied in the 2012 Santangelo study, *A Phenomenological Inquiry into the Financial Education Experience of Young, Low-Income Credit Union Members.*   The 2012 Santangelo study focuses explicitly on the lived experience of participants as their perceived behavioral changes in the areas of savings, cash, and credit management, and includes the identification of four key steps associated with transformative learning. The exploration of the lived learning experiences among study participants in this context-rich, non-formal educational environment sought to reveal themes and expose evidence of a previously unexplored nature. During this journey, the themes suggested a set of teaching and learning sequences that when properly applied to a financial education experience may enhance the likelihood of changed personal financial management behaviors and exposed evidence of transformative learning.

Using a semi-structured interview protocol, and engaging 20 study participants, the Santangelo (2012) study included insights into the personal financial adult-learning experience of young, low-income adult credit union members at The Denver Community Credit Union. The intent of this study was to (a) develop deeper understandings about what triggers changes in personal financial management behaviors in the areas of savings, credit, and cash management; and (b) sought to identify evidence of transformational learning among participants. The study incorporated a transcendental phenomenological design to discover what was previously unseen. The qualitative method suited this study well because the research questions incorporated the pursuit of a deeper understanding and explored data in the form of words.

Qualitative research methods are different from quantitative research methods in several significant ways. First, qualitative research methods incorporate the collection of data in the form of words and pictures and not numbers (Leedy & Ormron, 2010). Next, the qualitative researcher is seeking meaningful insight or deeper understanding, and the quantitative researcher is seeking to compare, examine, and evaluate data in the form of numbers.

These deeper understandings generated using a qualitative method result from the exploration of a key concept or idea and focus on a central phenomenon (Creswell, 2007). Transcendental phenomenology is a qualitative study design used to develop a new understanding known as the universal essence of a given phenomenon. According to Moustakas (1994), "phenomenology refers to the knowledge as it appears to consciousness, the science of describing what one perceives, senses, and knows in one's immediate awareness and experience" (p. 26). Knowledge garnered through phenomenological inquiry emphasizes intuition and essence which precedes empirical knowledge (Kockelmans, 1967).

Subtleties in Phenomenology

Approaches to the process of phenomenological inquiry are subtle but important for clear understanding. Researchers often use many approaches when conducting a phenomenological inquiry, but for those just in the beginning stages of understanding how this study design functions, a limited discussion is most useful. This chapter includes a limited focus and briefly explores the distinctions between three key phenomenological approaches. These approaches include hermeneutic phenomenology, interpretive phenomenological analysis (IPA), and transcendental phenomenology. The Santangelo (2012) study included the application of transcendental phenomenology and therefore the majority of the material discussed in this chapter emphasizes the transcendental design.

According to Moustakas (1994), transcendental phenomenology is distinct from other forms of phenomenology because "it adheres to what can be discovered through reflection on subjective acts and their objective correlates" (p. 45). Subjective acts are not empirical and emphasize someone's feelings, perceptions, or opinions. Objective correlates, however, are free from bias, consist of facts, and are exempt from influence by feeling and perception (Moustakas). The act of describing the relationships between the subjective and the objective within the phenomenon results in the essence or universal understanding of a given phenomenon. Later in this chapter, two key data analysis techniques known as textual and structural descriptions provide context to the notion of describing both the subjective and the objective and how this results in deeper understanding and insight when employing a transcendental phenomenological design. The next two phenomenological approaches worthy of further exploration included both interpretative and hermeneutical phenomenology. Hermeneutical phenomenology is different from transcendental phenomenology, but still contains many of the distinguishing characteristics of the phenomenological study design.

Hermeneutical phenomenology is often thought of in relation to understanding and interpreting biblical texts (Smith, Flowers, & Larkin, 2009). Since the late 1920s, however, researchers expanded and applied this important technique to a much broader set of texts. Hermeneutical phenomenology explores the relationships that link the context of the text's construction with the context of the interpretation of the text (Smith et al., 2009). One key approach includes the focus on the exact and objective meaning of the text under analysis and the comparison of this text with the individuality of an author's voice (Schleiermacher, 1998). Similar to hermeneutic phenomenology, interpretative phenomenology explores the relationship between what is seen and what is perceived.

Interpretative phenomenological analysis is more deeply dependent on the researcher than both transcendental and hermeneutical phenomenology. Unlike other types of phenomenology discussed, IPA has two equally important axes. The first is the exploration of significant events in the lives of people aimed to help make sense of these experiences. The second is the interpretation of these experiences by the researcher to reveal a newly understood insight. This interpretation helps a researcher understand how the participant makes sense of the significant experience under exploration (Smith et al., 2009). The differences between transcendental, hermeneutical, and interpretive phenomenology can be both small and subtle, but recognizing these small differences is instrumental when the novice researcher attempts to match the research questions to the study design. Once a clear understanding of phenomenology is in place, it is easier to understand how to determine the appropriateness or 'fit' of the study design to the nature of the study.

The Appropriateness of the Study Design

The Santangelo (2012) study included the exploration of a significant experience in the lives of an experientially homogenous study group, and the researcher sought to identify feelings, perceptions, and opinions that present themselves as evidence resulting from the participants' own awareness. The transcendental phenomenological design was appropriate because the researcher endeavored to reduce the participants' experiences with the phenomenon of financial education to one description representing the universal essence. Phenomenology involves an exploration of experience as a means to obtain comprehensive descriptions based on reflective textual and structural analysis that portray the essence of the experience (Moerer-Urdahl & Creswell, 2004). In the Santangelo study, phenomenological design was appropriate for examining, organizing, and categorizing the reported experiences of young, low-income credit union members after participants experienced change in their personal financial management behaviors. Enhanced validity is a primary element of the Santangelo 2012 study because the knowledge sought occurred through a comprehensive description of the collected data. According to Moustakas (1994), "Scientific investigation is valid when the knowledge sought is arrived at through descriptions that make possible an understanding of the meaning and essences of experience" (p. 84). The Santangelo 2012 study fits the study design well because the researcher focused on describing the experience under study rather than interpreting the experience. Learners seeking to understand how to test the fit or appropriateness of a study and match that fit to transcendental phenomenology must keep this important test in mind. According to Sokolowski (2000b), studies that focus on the description of the experience of the participants and less on the interpretations of the experience by the researcher are consistent with the foundations of transcendental phenomenology.

Understanding the appropriateness or fit of a study to its study methodology and design is both a labor of science and one of art. When a novice researcher examines a study prospectus for clues about the best design, the learner should apply several tests or ask several important questions. These tests or questions should yield the following answers when the prospectus is appropriate for using transcendental phenomenology. First, the phenomenon under study should explore a significant experience in the lives of the study participants. A significant experience is one that affects the lives of the people involved in such a way that changes the actions, understandings, perceptions, presuppositions, or behaviors of those experiencing the phenomenon (Smith et al., 2009). Next, the group under study should be experientially homogenous. Study participants should have had the same or a very similar experience and must meet certain specific criteria e.g. gender, age, and other conditions (Creswell, 2009). If the study prospectus aims at exploring a phenomenon with the intent to describe rather than interpret the experience, the study will likely pass one of the tests that will distinguish the study as a transcendental phenomenological exploration (Moustakas, 1994). Finally, if the prospectus incorporates a detailed description of the experience under exploration, this measure will both enhance the validity of the study and comply with the descriptive nature of transcendental phenomenology. According to Moustakas (1994), a comparison of the objective and subjective descriptions of the phenomenon is an elemental component of transcendental phenomenology and is one pathway for generating the universal essence of the phenomenon.

Data Collection and Instrumentation

Interviews are a common way of collecting qualitative data while conducting a transcendental phenomenological study. Interviews are a useful way of discovering meaningful patterns that describe particular phenomenon and help the researcher arrive at the heart of the matter (Leedy & Ormron, 2010). A data collection process that underscores or supports the key activity of describing the phenomenon under study is consistent with the foundations of transcendental phenomenology (Moustakas, 1994). According to Creswell (2007), both interviews and formal written responses are appropriate forms for collecting phenomenological data. The Santangelo (2012) study employed both these elements.

The interviews conducted as part of the Santangelo (2012) study were via telephone and recorded using a digital recording device and a speakerphone. According to Sturges (2004), telephone interviews can provide the best form of data when the researcher cannot readily access study participants in person. Each participant also responded to a set of written questions designed to gain detailed information the interviews might miss, and to provide an element of privacy for participants. Creswell (2005) asserted that formal written responses are among the data collection instruments commonly used in a phenomenological design. Personal financial management is a private and under-discussed topic that could prove to be embarrassing for some participants. The participants in the Santangelo study were more frank and direct about their personal financial management behaviors than they were during the interview process because of the privacy inherent in the read-and-respond interview format (Santangelo, 2012). Developing the interview instrumentation in a way that is consistent with transcendental phenomenology is also an important part of the study design.

Collecting data using interview and read-respond questions under the rubric of transcendental phenomenology must aim at identifying the participants' perceptions, feelings, and emotions as they experienced the phenomenon (Moustakas, 1994). Inexperienced researchers may find themselves tempted to permit the study design to rule the structure of the interview questions. Some element of each question should be consistent with the study design, but research questions should act as the primary guide for developing the interview instrument (Van Manen, 1990). Research questions designed for consistency with transcendental phenomenology should also yield insight into the perceptions, emotions, and feelings of the study participants.

The Santangelo (2012) study incorporated the exploration of both feelings and perceptions, and this is evident in both the research questions and the data collection questions. A list of the data collection questions can be found in Appendix B of the Santangelo study. The following interview question is a good example of a phenomenological data collection tool. "As a result of your recent class at Denver Community Credit Union, what new feelings and perceptions about your own money management habits have emerged?" (Santangelo, 2012, p. 76). This question incorporates both feelings and perceptions as the participants reflect upon the phenomenon under study. The following research question also aligns with the constructs of transcendental phenomenology. This question incorporates the perceptions of study participants. "What adult financial education experiences are perceived by the study participants to support higher savings levels, improve credit scores, and enhance cash flow among young, low-income adults?" (Santangelo, 2012, p. 15). The data collection instruments in addition to aligning with the fundamental principles of the study design must demonstrate the foundations of reliability and validity.

Research instruments should provide the readers with confidence that they are stable and consistent (Creswell, 2005). Qualitative reliability is one way to foster stability and should focus on consistency of the outcomes that result from a well-designed data collection instrument (Lewis, 2009). The Santangelo (2012) study employed the test-retest reliability method. Lewis also asserted that a test-retest reliability method requires asking participants to review their responses and confirm the accuracy of their responses at a later date. Another common way to further enhance reliability is to use a pilot study (Neuman, 2006). According to Kim (2011), pilot studies consist of a small group of participants that represent the characteristics of the study population. Kim further explained that pilot study populations can provide feedback on interview questions in a phenomenological study; however, pilot participants cannot be a part of the main study. Enhanced reliability occurred in the Santangelo study through the incorporation of a pilot study. Reliability and validity are relevant research concepts that when considered together enhance the accuracy of a study.

The Santangelo (2012) study incorporated the use of internal, external, and intersubjective validity. Intersubjective validity uses the concept of pre-established harmonies and emphasizes the idea of reciprocal actions (Gardner, 2005). Employing multiple methods of data gathering combined with triangulation strengthens the internal validity of a qualitative study (Creswell, 2009). The Santangelo study incorporated the use of multiple data gathering methods by applying both a one-on-one telephone interview and a formal written interview approach. The Santangelo study also applied triangulation by using collaborative evidence gathered from two data gathering sources, including interviews and a formal written read-and-respond strategy. According to Creswell (2005), "Qualitative inquiries triangulate among different data sources to enhance the accuracy of a study" (p. 252). Once the data collection instruments are in place and after data collection occurs, the researcher should focus next on data analysis.

Data Analysis: The Heart of Transcendental Phenomenology

The data analysis phase under the transcendental phenomenological study design is also common to other phenomenological designs in that it involves organizing and synthesizing data into groups, clusters, and themes in an effort to build the description of the phenomenon. These groups, clusters, and themes act as the building blocks for the description known as the universal essence. The first step of the analytical process is coding data. A *coding* process organizes the text of the transcripts and results in the discovery of data patterns. Within the organizational structure of the transcript, general categories create a system of data known as open coding. Next, the researcher must position the categories within the theoretical model (axial coding); and finally, explicating a story from the interconnections of these categories (selective coding) (Creswell, 2009). Once coding is complete, a seven-phase process of data analysis begins. This process is unique to transcendental phenomenology and is known as the modified van Kaam approach (Moustakas, 1994).

The first phase of data analysis incorporating the modified van Kaam model generally consists of finding and listing statements about how participants were experiencing the phenomenon (Moustakas, 1994). This process is known as horizontalization (Giorgi, 2006). The Santangelo (2012) study focused on how the participants were experiencing changes in their own financial management behaviors. The second phase of data analysis ensures that all these statements have both equal worth and equal weight. This step involves the development of a list of non-repetitive, non-overlapping statements. The third phase of data analysis identifies the invariant constituents. According to Moustakas (1994), invariant constituents fulfill two requirements: (a) invariant constituents must contain a phenomenological moment of the experience necessary and significant to understanding the experience; and (b) invariant constituents must comply to the process of abstraction and labeling. Phenomenological moments cannot stand apart independently from the whole to which the moment belongs (Sokolowski, 2000a).

The fourth phase of the data analysis process involves clustering the invariant constituents into larger thematic units. These groups represent the core themes of the experience (Moustakas, 1994). The fifth phase of the data analysis process involves creating an individual textual description of the experience describing what happened and includes verbatim examples. The sixth phase of the data analysis process includes a written description of how the experience happened; this is known as structural descriptions (Moerer-Urdahl & Creswell, 2004). The seventh and final phase of data analysis captures the essence of the experience by writing a composite description that incorporates both the textual and structural descriptions.

The composite descriptions are the core of the universal essence and the distinguishing hallmark of transcendental phenomenology. The composite description represents a thoughtfully articulated construction and consists of two components. The first component is a short, simply and clearly written statement describing how the participants experienced the phenomenon known as the textual description, derived verbatim from the invariant constituents, and recorded in the words of the participant whenever possible. The second component is a more descriptive construct and focuses on what the participant experienced while undergoing the phenomenon. This construct, known as the structural description, contains more of the researchers own words and occurs in a more detailed and elaborate format than its counterpart—the textual description. The composite description reveals both the what— derived from the textual description, and the how—derived from the structural description. These two elements create the foundation for the objective and subjective descriptions identified earlier in this chapter. The objective element known as the textual description represents what is, while the structural description provides insight into the subjective nature of the phenomenon, what is seen.

These two elements when combined to form one description, known as the composite description, represent the universal essence of the phenomena under study. The universal essence—the illustrative structure resulting from the composite description— provides the foundation used to construct study recommendations, provide insights and conclusions, and in the case of the Santangelo (2012) study, act as the fundamental building block for the study outcomes. The outcomes of the Santangelo study included a set of teaching and learning sequences and a descriptive model illustrating the educational pathway designed to increase the likelihood of fundamental personal financial management behavioral changes experienced by the study participants. The teaching and learning sequences and the descriptive model are in the original Santangelo dissertation.

Summary

In this chapter, an overview of the qualitative method and the transcendental phenomenological design provides a step-by-step study protocol through the lens of the Santangelo (2012) study. The chapter includes the explanation of the data collection protocol. The two key data collection strategies described in this chapter include telephone interviews using a one-on-one interview approach, and formal read-and-respond questions using an individual short-answer approach. Personal financial management learning experiences can be difficult for participants to explain in a one-on-one interview setting because the information is confidential and can be embarrassing. This chapter, therefore, includes the information on the nature of participant confidentiality.

This chapter employs the examination and explanation of the reliability and validity of the data collection instruments. A pilot study described in the chapter helped to enhance reliability of the Santangelo (2012) study; and triangulation, described in this chapter, explained how enhanced validity occurs under the rubric of transcendental phenomenology. The chapter also includes an examination of internal, external and *intersubjective validity* (Moustakas, 1994 p. 51). This chapter also incorporates the examination and description of the data analysis protocol using a modified van Kaam structure commonly seen in a transcendental phenomenological inquiry.

References

Creswell, J. W. (2005). *Educational research: Planning, conducting, and evaluating quantitative and qualitative research* (2nd ed.). Upper Saddle River, NJ: Merrill Prentice-Hall.

Creswell, J. W. (2007). *Qualitative inquiry & research design: Choosing among five approaches* (2nd ed.). Thousand Oaks, CA: Sage.

Creswell, J. W. (2009). *Research design: Qualitative, quantitative, and mixed method approaches* (3rd ed.). Thousand Oaks, CA: Sage.

Gardner, S. (2005). Sartre, intersubjectivity, and German idealism. *Journal of the History of Philosophy, 43*, 325-351. doi:10.1353/hph.2005.0135

Giorgi, A. (2006). Concerning variations in the application of the phenomenological method. *Humanistic Psychologist, 34*, 305-319. doi:10.1207/s15473333thp3404_2

Kim, Y. (2011). The pilot study in qualitative inquiry: Identifying issues and learning lessons for culturally competent research. *Qualitative Social Work, 10*(2), 190-206. doi:10.1177/1473325010362001

Kockelmans, J. J. (1967). *Phenomenology*. Garden City, NY: Doubleday.

Leedy, P. D., & Ormron, J. E. (2010). *Practical research: Planning and design* (9th ed.). Upper Saddle River, NJ: Pearson.

Lewis, J. (2009). Redefining qualitative methods: Believability in the fifth moment. *International Journal of Qualitative Methods, 8*(2), 1-14. http://ejournals.library.ualberta.ca/index.php/IJQM/index

Moerer-Urdahl, T., & Creswell, J. W. (2004). Using transcendental phenomenology to explore the "Rippel Effect" in a leadership mentoring program. *International Journal of Qualitative Methods, 3*(2), 19-35. http://ejournals.library.ualberta.ca/index.php/IJQM/index

Moustakas, C. (1994). *Phenomenological research methods*. Thousand Oaks, CA: Sage.

Neuman, W. L. (2006). *Social research methods: Qualitative and quantitative approaches* (6th ed.). Upper Saddle River, NJ: Prentice Hall.

Santangelo, D. J. (2012). *A phenomenological inquiry into the financial education experience of young, low-income, credit union members* (Doctoral dissertation). Retrieved from ProQuest Dissertations & Theses database. (UMI No. 3533761)

Schleiermacher, F. (1998). *Hermeneutics and criticism and other writings.* Cambridge, UK: CUP.

Smith, J. A., Flowers, P., & Larkin, M. (2009). *Interpretative phenomenological analysis.* Thousand Oaks, CA: Sage.

Sokolowski, R. (2000a). *Introduction to phenomenology.* New York, NY: Cambridge University Press.

Sokolowski, R. (2000b). Transcendental phenomenology. *Modern Philosophy, 7*(1), 233-241. doi:10.5840/wcp202000763

Sturges, J. E. (2004). Comparing telephone and face-to-face qualitative interviews: A research note. *Qualitative Research, 4*(1), 107-118. doi:10.1177/1468794104041110

Van Manen, M. (1990). *Researching lived experiences: Human science for an action sensitive pedagogy.* Albany, NY: State University of New York Press.

About the Author...

Denver Colorado author Dr. Daniel J. Santangelo holds several accredited degrees including, a Bachelor of Science (BS) From Regis University; Master of Arts (MA) from the University of Denver, School of Education; and a Doctorate of Education in Adult Learning Theory (Ed.D.) from the University of Phoenix, School of Advanced Studies.

Dr. Dan, as his clients and colleagues know him, is an association executive, serving as Senior Vice President of Association Services and the Executive Director of the Mountain West Credit Union Foundation. Dr. Santangelo is an adult curriculum design expert, and is a nationally recognized speaker and trainer. Dr. Dan serves as an executive performance coach, and specializes in distance education in non-formal adult training settings, grant writing, and developing multi-media and distance-based training and education programs for a wide range of adult learners.

Published work includes his dissertation *A Phenomenological Inquiry into the Financial Education Experience of Young, Low-Income Credit Union Members.*

To reach Dr. Daniel Santangelo for information on adult learning, executive coaching, and curriculum design write him at dansantangelo@aol.com

CHAPTER 10

Moving Through the Great Recession (2007-2009):
Personal Knowledge Management for Employment
Opportunity

by Dr. Susie Schild

O rganizations do not know what their most valuable assets
know, which creates risk to a business in a competitive
global economy (Mclean, 2009). This chapter provides
a blueprint for becoming more aware of employee knowledge
capital and using that knowledge to increase the success of a
business. By telling the story of workers' experiences with personal
knowledge management, the Schild (2013) study helped fill a gap
in research and literature. Insights gained from this study create
an advantage for leaders who, after reading this chapter, will have
a sense of the opportunities for success that are waiting now inside
their organization. For the new researcher, there is something
here for you as well. When the path of the research journey seems
unclear in light of the numerous things learned on the journey
and knowing that much more is unknown, the highlights of this
study regarding qualitative methods can act as a guide.

The birth of this study came from maximizing a chance
opportunity. The opportunity to work for the Department
of the Army on a knowledge management project launched

the Schild (2013) study, *Personal Knowledge Management for Employee Commoditization.* The initial literature review offered the organizational and technology perspective of knowledge management. After 2 years of research, a specific blog post sharpened the research focus on the employee perspective of knowledge management. McGee's (2003) blog post proposed that flawed knowledge management thinking resulted in the perception that the organization was the primary beneficiary of knowledge; however, people create knowledge not organizations, and thus, the primary benefactor is the person who creates the knowledge.

Moving Through the Great Recession (2007-2009): Personal Knowledge Management for Employment Opportunity

Overview of the Study

A review of literature revealed limited research on personal knowledge management, which meant an understanding of the knowledge workers' circumstances in an organizations' environment was also limited (Aaron, 2009; Austin, 2008; McLean, 2009; Pauleen, 2009). A lack of understanding for the personal knowledge management experience strengthened the argument for a qualitative study used to discover people's opinions and understandings of a specific situation (Leedy & Ormrod, 2010; Shank, 2006). The framework constructed set limitations for this study, which included knowledge management, personal knowledge management, symbolic capital, and generational theory. The inclusion of knowledge management gave a broad background from which to base the Schild (2013) study. Personal knowledge management allowed the study to focus on people's individual experiences and beliefs about their own knowledge management.

The inclusion of generational theory allowed for the perceptions of the generations currently in the workforce. Participant views on the value of personal knowledge emerged using the four forms of symbolic capital theory: economic, cultural, social, and symbolic. Perception, influence, and recognition granted by a person places a value on a form of capital (Bourdieu, 1998). Research suggests the value in personal knowledge management for organizations is increased employee knowledge, which organizations use to compete for sustainable advantage (Świgoń, 2011). Kao (2010) suggested that the value of personal knowledge is the ability to make decisions that forward personal agendas.

Background

Knowledge management begins with Frederick Taylor, founder of scientific management, who optimized work processes of manual production workers (Drucker, 1974). Implementing knowledge of standardized processes as a means to increase profits is one organizational benefit. The perspective of the organization as the primary beneficiary of knowledge becomes clear. With clear benefits to an organization, a means to capture the knowledge of individuals has been the subject of knowledge management studies (Aaron, 2009; Austin, 2008; Crawford, 2005; Nonaka & Takeuchi, 1995; Stankosky, 2005; Vasconcelos, 2007). The task of capturing knowledge continues to be difficult and part of the reason for this might be understood through the lens of knowledge management that remains a complex and often intangible concept. A comprehensive study of 1,182 resources found that no model described or encompassed the diverse concept of knowledge management (Onions, 2010). A reason why knowledge management remains abstract, which further supported the purpose of this study came from, Haller (2010), T. Karrer, (personal communication, March 12, 2012), J. McGee (personal communication, March 14, 2012), and Pauleen (2009) who suggested that little research is available that focuses on individuals' perspectives of personal knowledge management.

Stankosky (2005) revealed a connection between personal knowledge and the economy by proposing that knowledge is the primary provider of currency in a global economy and a commodity produced and owned by knowledge workers. The knowledge economy increases the importance of people's *know how* skills; meaning, knowledge holds a dollar value (Enz, 2010). Global industries leaders recognize that workers need improved *know how* and creative skills in the workforce to increase available jobs and succeed in a knowledge economy (OECD, 2010).

Maximizing benefits to people, businesses, communities, and general knowledge in society requires input from knowledge workers to understand what will make them successful in organizational culture (Aaron, 2009; Austin, 2008; McLean, 2009; Pauleen, 2009). Haller (2010), and Pauleen and Gorman, (2011) advocate that as a means of career and life management, personal knowledge includes leveraging information, achieving personal goals, and relating experiences. Chase (1997) stated that a survey performed by *The Journal of Knowledge Management*, found 76% of participants believed that knowledge management strategies should focus on people, which gave one more reason for the Schild (2013) study to focus on personal knowledge management.

Background research for this study indicated connections to symbolic capital theory. One indicator that symbolic capital has a connection to personal knowledge management was a lack of mutual understanding, which presents difficulties when leaders try to make use of the "know how" workers express (Austin, 2008; Murray & Newman, 2010). Mutual understanding that includes common language and knowledge are involved in social activities that include the workplace. Lin (2007) suggested the strength of common language and mutual understanding for knowledge management are the benefits perceived through the act of sharing knowledge and is self-motivating. Perceived benefits of knowledge sharing are enhanced organizational outcomes and competitive advantage, which is a goal of organizational leaders (McLean, 2009; Vasconcelos, 2007).

Theory

This research study provided insights into the personal knowledge management experience of 21 knowledge workers considering four forms of capital: (a) economic, (b) cultural, (c) social, and (d) symbolic. The conceptual framework developed for the purpose of this study included four ideas: (a) knowledge management, (b) symbolic capital, (c) personal knowledge management, and (c) generational theory. The literature review for this study indicated a conceptual versus a theoretical approach was a good fit for the subject of personal knowledge management. Readers may also wonder why these four ideas comprise the conceptual framework. Offered in the following two paragraphs is a summary highlighting pieces of the literature review that helped guide the formation of the conceptual framework.

Onions (2010) suggested viewing knowledge management not as an explicit theory, but instead as a body of knowledge or from a conceptual approach. Personal knowledge management evolved conceptually similar to the concept of knowledge management, in which both encompass a broad array of approaches, tools, activities, solutions, theories, and techniques, which may explain why a lack of conceptual development exists (Pauleen, 2009; Pauleen & Gorman, 2011). The concept of personal knowledge management combines diverse fields such as knowledge management, personal information management, philosophy, management science, cognitive psychology, and communications (Pauleen, 2009).

A focus on the current workforce made generational theory a logical inclusion. From a sociological position, generational theory provides meaning and an understanding of the drivers behind people's behavior (Codrington, 2008; Joshi et al., 2010; Strauss & Howe, 1991). A person seeks competitive advantage with their personal knowledge (Pauleen, 2009). Bourdieu (1977) suggested symbolic capital dictates the value of knowledge based on appreciation and perception, negotiated and supported by people to facilitate socioeconomic activities. For example, task assignment demonstrates valued knowledge established by the social complexity of an organization, which paints a picture of symbolic capital in practice. Symbolic capital resides in people and provides a lens for social exchange (Bourdieu, 1998). The theory of symbolic capital closely aligns with the theory of situated cognition, which describes how an individual learns from external experiences, the individual's internal awareness, images of the world, and symbolic exchanges with society (Robbins & Aydede, 2009). To summarize, symbolic capital affects personal knowledge management experiences across the generational workforce. The findings from the literature review supported the construction of the conceptual framework.

Focus on Data Analysis Methodology

The qualitative methods used in the Schild (2013) study includes interviews gathered from 21 knowledge workers that were members of the popular professional networking site, LinkedIn. These 21 contributors explained their opinions and understandings of personal knowledge management through interviews. Several reasons made using LinkedIn useful for this study. Knowledge workers, distinctly different from the production-oriented worker, perform "tasks where scanning for new information or knowledge inside or outside of the organization leads to knowledge creation"

(Chen & Edginton, 2005, p. 281). A review of the LinkedIn community demographics information suggested that members were very likely knowledge workers, performing various types of work that did not include manual labor. Community members' profiles represented a broad array of industries and job types. A representation of four generations of knowledge workers existed within the community. Finally, the use of a social media platform would serve as a virtual place to gather data, which integrated the use of technology, would push the limits of traditional research methods, and include the learning's from years spent studying channels to connect technology and education.

A 12 question semi-structured interview served as the data collection instrument. One reason for the selection of the semi-structured interview was that the interview is an effective method of data collection (Bystad, Fylkenses, Oleke, & Tumwine, 2007). The interview method of data collection allows participants to share how their everyday lives reflect a specific phenomenon (Leedy & Ormrod, 2010). Another reason was the interview method produced a transcript needed for the data analysis procedure. The data analysis procedure was a modified van Kaam method by Moustakas (1994) using NVivo 10$^{©}$ software. The modified van Kaam method by Moustakas' (1994) is a seven-step approach that exposes participant experiences allowing themes to emerge which are relevant across participant experiences. NVivo$^{©}$ was particularly useful to discover emergent themes in the transcripts and to verify contributing factors to themes through participant biographies.

In more than one way, the approach to acquiring the data used in this study was a unique experience. Currently, community blog sites store doctoral students' experiences of struggling to obtain Internal Review Board (IRB) approval, using LinkedIn as a population, which is a similar experience encountered with the

Schild (2013) research study. LinkedIn and other social media venues exist as available options for the doctoral student and researcher. To gain IRB approval, understand the culture of the network community chosen for the population for research and communicate the right message to the IRB. The Schild (2013) dissertation contains specifics of how to document properly the use of a LinkedIn as a virtual space to recruit research participants and receive IRB approval. A suggestion for researchers considering using LinkedIn is to engage with the Internet communities. Connecting with community members will help achieve research goals in ways not imagined.

During the data collection phase, one *Aha* moment as a researcher and knowledge worker was experiencing the power of networking, which translated through marketing the study and building relationships to gain the data needed (Schild, 2013). This data collection experience was unexpected, yet tied neatly into the findings of this study. Analyzing the data proved to be a challenge with the verbatim method of transcription. During the 21 interviews, only one participant spoke without the significant use of filler words such as Ah, You Know, and Um. Sifting through the extraneous words proved to be time consuming; however, the use of software such as NVivo© was helpful attaining the data sought. NVivo© software is particularly suited to transcriptions as a data set. The learning to share here is to carefully review the types of transcription methods accepted in research and consider how the different methods will benefit analysis, software, and data output.

NVivo 10© software parsed the data from the transcriptions for analysis. However, the research process uncovered similar products for transcription free of charge and without a time restriction. Eliminating the potential expiration of a trial version of software and the expense of having to purchase a product may be an advantage to academic and industry researchers. Additional resources found useful with qualitative data in the transcription process were applications found on smart phones and computers. Voice-to-text software, digital recorders, and audio conversion software were some of the technology considerations that proved advantageous as well.

A final note on data analysis not often discussed is the value of a pilot study. Pilot studies require analysis and from that analysis, improvements to a study's outcome are possible (Shuttleworth, 2010). Without a test run of the interview questions, the data in this research study would not have obtained the resulting quality. Analyzing the data in the pilot study resulted in a changed approach to asking questions, which included eliminating and rephrasing of questions. The pilot study offered the opportunity to try different technologies with qualitative data. The recommendation to new researchers is try different technologies throughout your doctoral journey. The effort of technology exploration paid rich dividends for the efforts of becoming a more informed researcher.

Findings

Participants from across generational and geographic boundaries engaged in work across varied industries and provided examples of their personal knowledge management experience that produced four themes: (a) stay current, (b) access to people, (c) knowledge sharing, and (d) situational knowledge (Schild, 2013). From the transcribed interviews, descriptions were produced that added to the understanding of the personal knowledge management experience. Four themes appeared from the interview data. Activities such as networking, resources, and mentors contributed to the larger themes. Knowledge sharing is one theme produced from the interviews. Participants believed that specific activities and resources were important to maintaining and acquiring workplace advantage and validated the connection to symbolic capital theory used in this study. Validating the attributes of the themes produced by participant interviews occurred through a comparison of participant personal profiles. This meant that what the participants stated in the interview, which translated into the themes though data analysis, was reflected in their public profiles. Each theme has associated components for which participants attributed value and believed contributed to their employability, growth, learning, and personal knowledge management.

The unexpected global event which unfolded during this research study, often referred to as, *The Great Recession,* spanned across the years 2007through 2009 (Coy, 2012). A thought occurred as the data were analyzed, which was *The Great Recession* could have influenced ecological validity of the findings in the Schild (2013) study. The ability to prove this effect may not be possible, however; considering the numerous and pervasive effects of this economic landslide, understandably, the beliefs of participants regarding how their personal knowledge affects employability could now be different than prior to 2007. The economic effects, if they exist, might not be equal across generations, geographical boundaries, industries, or job types. These effects would be part of the experiences of knowledge workers and a consideration for leaders trying to understand their employees' personal knowledge management that affects the value of knowledge capital in an organization. Events that are individual or far reaching like *The Great Recession* affect the human experience and researchers should consider how both influence study results. Thinking outside the box, the effects of *The Great Recession* on personal knowledge management might be a consideration for future study.

Ingrained and interconnected, characteristics of the human experience do not strictly begin and end, but rather stream fluidly. Interconnected themes presented themselves through analysis.

As the data unfolded, themes fluidly presented. These themes mirrored the interrelated connections across forms of capital in the conceptual framework. This validation was a decisive moment, which signaled that the mechanics of the conceptual framework operated dependably for this research study. Understanding that the study's framework and findings were cohesive, a new challenge posed itself. The challenge was thinking how to present the interrelated themes through the linear approach of the dissertation. Constructing a presentation emerged through reaching out to communities of interest, personal networks, reviewing prior research, community of practice discussions, and open dialogue with peers and mentors. Asking for opinions, ideas, and feedback provided a platform for knowledge and information sharing through which the fabric of a new creation materialized. The lesson learned was to move away from examples of data presentation that were not sufficient for telling the story the data from the Schild (2013) provided and construct something different and purposeful. A meaningful approach to presenting qualitative research data now serves as an example to help other researchers in the Schild (2013) study.

An interesting finding was the absence of technology as a major theme across generations considering the pervasiveness of technology. Sentiments of 21 participants regarding technology emerged through the statement of one participant who stated that technology was a means to get to what was needed; acquiring personal knowledge was not about technology (Schild, 2013). Silent Generation participants did not discuss technology as an important personal knowledge management consideration. Generational differences were not a factor for engagement in personal knowledge management activities, which supported current academic generational research.

Mentioned earlier was the power of networking and relationship building that was a driving factor in the completion of the Schild (2013) study. The experiences of participants revealed networking and relationship building as activities necessary for successful personal knowledge management. These same activities were necessary to collect the required data for this study. Not only did the success of this study rely on a personal foundation with LinkedIn community members, the networking capacity of that foundation had to be mobilized. The need to mobilize the foundational network became clear once the initial call for participants posted in the community groups and they did not come! Active participation was required to create awareness of the need for study participants. Events during the research process proved the involvement of community members was contingent on the familiarity of the relationship. Relationships matter and these community members went into their network and spread the word about this research study. The participation of LinkedIn members who promoted this study was valuable and an interesting process to examine. The opportunity to reflect on the findings from this study in relation to the research experience brought further validation to the data. The validation was having realized that the researcher had lived a similar experience and employed some of the same activities as relayed by this study's participants throughout the research process. The experience was personal knowledge management in action.

Conclusion

Individuals benefit from the findings of this study in multiple ways, which include: insight into the knowledge shared by knowledge workers who explained how they manage their knowledge; the perceived needs for a successful knowledge management process, and how 21 participants understood the constantly changing process of their personal knowledge management in an effort remain employable. The Schild (2013) research study has significance to leaders in education through the indications that educators are integral to the improvement of knowledge management processes and serve as resources to improve the learning and functional skills needed by students to prepare them for workforce participation. Leaders are provided an example of the value of a bottom up approach to building and sharing corporate knowledge and benefit the future success of a business. The findings from this current research study allows leaders to consider factors that drive personal knowledge management to improve organizational opportunities, support personal knowledge management activities, assist knowledge workers to attain leadership qualities, and understand knowledge worker value propositions. This research provides leaders, individuals, and society with information aligned to the production of citizens better able to compete in a global economy.

The research process provided the opportunity to think outside the box. Figuring out a way to obtain IRB approval was a refractive process. With limited information to triangulate findings, an approach different from anything known to the researcher had to be created. Thinking outside the box involved deciding to depart from available examples of data presentation to construct something that told the personal knowledge management story. Seeking professional opinions from those currently involved in knowledge management to assist in validating this personal knowledge management study was daring and exciting. During the research process, refractive thinking pushed my professional and academic limits providing opportunities to become a more knowledgeable researcher with technology platforms to obtain and analyze data. Sharing my learning to improve organizational processes and help people manage their personal knowledge through organization and volunteer work during the Schild (2013) research study was an honor. The opportunity to support those currently constructing the dissertations of tomorrow has also been a pleasure. I look forward to being an active participant in the continued improvement of knowledge management processes in academics and industry.

References

Aaron, B. (2009). Determining the business impact of knowledge management. *Performance Improvement, 48*(4), 35-45. doi:10.1002/pfi.20060

Austin, M. (2008). Strategies for transforming human service organizations into learning organizations: Knowledge management and the transfer of learning. *Journal of Evidence Based Social Work, 5*(, 569-596. doi:10.1080/15433710802084326

Bystad, N., Fylkenses, K., Oleke, L., & Tumwine, J. K. (2007). Constraints of education opportunities of orphans: A community-based study from Northern Uganda. *AIDS Care, 19*, 361-368. doi:10.1080/09540120600677987

Bourdieu, P. (1977). *Outline of a theory of practice.* Cambridge, UK: Harvard University Press.

Bourdieu, P. (1991). *Language and symbolic power* (3rd ed., G. Raymond & M. Adamson, Trans.). Cambridge, MA: Harvard University Press. (Original work published 1982)

Bourdieu, P. (1998). *Practical reason: On the theory of action.* Stanford, CA: Stanford University Press.

Chase, R. L. (1997). The knowledge-based organization: An international survey. *The Journal of Knowledge Management, 1*(1), 38-49. doi:10.1108/EUM0000000004578

Codrington, G. (2008, July). Detailed introduction to generational theory. *Tomorrow Today*, 1-16. Retrieved from http://www.tomorrowtoday.uk.com/articles/pdf/TomorrowToday_detailed_intro_to_Generations.pdf

Coy, P. (2012). The great recession: An "affair" to remember. *Bloomberg Business Week Politics & Policy.* Retrieved from http://www.businessweek.com/articles/2012-10-11/the-great-recession-an-affair-to-remember

Chen, A., & Edginton, T. (2005). Assessing value in organizational knowledge creation: Considerations for knowledge workers. *Management Information Systems Quarterly, 29*(2), 279-309. Retrieved from http://aisel.aisnet.org/misq/vol29/iss2/6/

Crawford, C. (2005). Effects of transformational leadership and organizational position on knowledge management. *Journal of Knowledge Management, 9*(6), 6-16. doi:10.1108/13673270510629927

Enz, C. A. (2010). *Hospitality strategic management: Concepts and cases* (2nd ed.). Hoboken, NJ: John Wiley & Sons.

Haller, H. (2010, September 20). *PKM 2010—workshop slides* [Slideshow]. Retrieved from http://www.slideshare.net/heikohaller/pkm-2010-workshop-slides

Joshi, A., Dencker, J. C., Franz, G., & Martocchio, J. J. (2010). Unpacking generational identities in organizations. *Academy of Management Review, 35*, 392-414. doi:10.5465./AMR.2010.51141800

Kao, R. W. (2010). *Sustainable economy: Corporate, social and environmental responsibility*. Singapore: World Scientific. Retrieved from http://books.google.com

Leedy, P., & Ormrod, J. (2010). *Practical research: Planning and design* (9th ed.). Upper Saddle River, NJ: Merrill.

Lin, H. F. (2007). Knowledge sharing and firm innovation capability: An empirical study. *International Journal of Manpower, 28*, 315-332. doi:10.1108/01437720710755272

McGee, J. (2003, August 19). Manage the first derivative [Web log post]. Retrieved from http://www.mcgeesmusings.net/2003/08/19.html

McLean, J. (2009, April/May). Does your organisation know what it knows? *The British Journal of Administrative Management, 66*, 32-33. Retrieved from https://ifind.swan.ac.uk/discover/Record/457975

Moustakas, C. (1994). *Phenomenological research methods*. Thousand Oaks, CA: Sage.\

Nonaka, I., & Takeuchi, H. (1995). *The knowledge-creating company: How Japanese companies create the dynamics of innovation*. New York, NY: Oxford University Press.

Onions, P. E. W. (2010, September). *Umbrellas, alphabet soup and knowledge management theory.* Paper presented at the 11th European Conference on Knowledge Management (ECKM), Famalicão, Portugal. Retrieved from http://www.patrickonions.org/docs/academic/Onions%20(2010)%20Umbrellas%20and%20alphabet%20soup.pdf

Organisation for Economic Co-operation and Development. (2010, November). *Better financing for SMEs and entrepreneurs for job creation and growth* (Issues Paper No. 2). Paper presented at the "Bologna+10" High-Level Meeting on Lessons From the Global Crisis and the Way Forward to Job Creation and Growth, Paris, France. Retrieved from http://www.oecd.org/cfe/smesandentrepreneurship/46404374.pdf

Pauleen, D. J. (2009). Personal knowledge management: Putting the "person" back into the knowledge equation. *Online Information Review, 33*(2), 221-224. doi:10.1108/14684520910951177

Pauleen, D. J., & Gorman, G. E. (2011). The nature and value of personal knowledge management. In D. J. Pauleen & G. E. Gorman (Eds.), *Personal knowledge management: Individual, organizational, and social perspectives* (pp. 1-16). Surrey, UK: Grower.

Pinch, T.J., & Bijker, W.E. (2010). The social construction of facts and artifacts: Or how the sociology of science and sociology of technology might benefit each other. In W.E. Bijker, T.P. Hughes, & T. Pinch (Ed.), *The social construction of technological systems: New directions in the sociology and history of technology* (pp. 11-44) Cambridge, MA: Massachusetts Institute of Technology.

Robbins, P., & Aydede, M. (Ed.).(2009). *The Cambridge handbook of situated cognition.* New York, NY: Cambridge University Press.

Shank, G. (2006). *Qualitative research: A personal skills approach* (2nd ed.). Upper Saddle River, NJ: Pearson.

Shuttleworth, M. (2010). Pilot study. *Explorable.* Retrieved from http://explorable.com/pilot-study.html

Stankosky, M. (2005). Advances in knowledge management: University research toward an academic discipline. In M. Stankosky (Ed.), *Creating the discipline of knowledge management: The latest in university research* (pp. 1-14). Burlington, MA: Elsevier Butterworth-Heinemann.

Stewart, T. A. (1999). *Intellectual capital: The new wealth of organizations.* New York, NY: Doubleday.

Strauss, W., & Howe, N. (1991). *Generations: The history of America's future, 1584 to 2069.* New York, NY: William Morrow and Company. Retrieved from http://books.google.com

Świgoń, M. (2011). Personal knowledge management (PKM) and personal employability management (PEM): Concepts based on competences. *Proceedings of the European Conference on Intellectual Capital,* 432-438. Retrieved from http://books.google.com

Vasconcelos, A. (2007). Dilemmas in knowledge management. *Library Management, 29,* 422-443. doi:10.1108/01435120810869165

About the Author ...

Currently a resident of Southern California author Dr. Susie A. Schild holds several accredited degrees; a Bachelor of Arts (BA) from California State University Long Beach; a Master of Management (MM) from University of Phoenix; and a Doctorate of Education (Ed.D/ ET) in Educational Leadership with a specialization in Educational Technology from University of Phoenix School of Advanced Studies. She holds two Knowledge Management Certifications from Knowledge Management Professional Society.

Dr. Susie manages student service for Corinthian Colleges. Dr. Susie also serves as a volunteer with the American Society for Training and Development in Orange County California collaborating with trainers, organizational development consultants, and website designers to improve information and education to its members and local businesses.

To reach Dr. Susie Schild for information on *Personal Knowledge Management for Employee Commoditization* or questions regarding the doctoral journey, please contact her at http://www.linkedin. com/in/susanschild or e-mail: susanschild00@gmail.com

EPILOGUE

The Refractive Thinker®:
Our Greater Purpose: To Serve the Doctoral Student and Scholar

By Dr. Cheryl A. Lentz

As *The Refractive Thinker*® *Doctoral Anthology* series moves forward, questions continue to surface regarding the concept of refractive thinking, particularly regarding the higher purpose for writing this series to serve the needs of the doctoral student and scholar. These questions include: what is a refractive thinker®, how did the concept of refractive thinking begin, and what value does this add to the concept of *thinking* and *critical thinking* as related to the power of research and discovery of the doctoral scholar. This commentary provides an in-depth analysis of this dynamic perspective as we continue to expand our definition of the elusive refractive thinker and continue to contribute to the research efforts of the doctoral scholar to change the world through the power of research and the scholars' enlightened pen.

Who is a Refractive Thinker®?

The concept of *refractive thinking* first emerged when as a college professor, I concluded that the concept of critical thinking was incomplete. Teaching for more than 13 years, I invite our authors to consider that there is more than simply an either or dichotomy regarding the concept of thinking. If thinking is *inside* the box, and critical thinking is *outside* the box, what then is beyond this approach? Who are those among us that think beyond this dichotomy? Enter the **refractive thinker**.

A *refractive thinker* is someone who is insatiable with curiosity. These thinkers are not satisfied within current conventional parameters or the prevailing wisdom. They are frustrated by provincial thinking or analysis. They do not follow the crowd. Instead, the crowd follows *them*. They ask questions as they continue to dig deep in their pursuit of knowledge and understanding. They do not excel within the constraints of only an either/or option in which many believe there are only two options: *in the box* or *out of the box* boundaries. Instead of merely preferring to color outside the lines, refractive thinkers prefer to redefine the rules that constrain the lines, questioning the very structure and existence.

Refractive thinkers are often those individuals who create and innovate new business models, those who may forge new scientific discoveries, and those who offer never before held theories to try to explain existing or new phenomenon. They are the explorers of thought, the champions of problem solving, the pioneers of possibilities, those willing to ask the right questions that often take them—and those following them—in new and unchartered directions, believing that unchartered waters are worthy of research and future discovery. The refractive thinker is excited by limitless boundaries and the suspensions of rules. Refractive thinkers are the those first in their fields such as Sir Isaac Newton, Albert Einstein, Benjamin Franklin, Leonardo da Vinci, Mohandas Gandhi, and Madame Curie to name but a few. The authors in this volume proudly follow in these footsteps, whereas refractive thinkers they not only ask *why*, but also *why not*.

Our Higher Purpose

As in the words of Peter Senge (1990), we cannot put new ideas into old constructs. With new paths that refractive thinkers forge, our role is to serve the needs of future doctoral students, faculty, as well as scholars, to help shorten their learning curve based on the lessons and knowledge learned by those who have traveled ahead of them.

With more than 70 authors from the around the globe as part of this collaboration, the goal of this collaboration is to offer the guidance and wisdom of contributions to the body of knowledge in a variety of fields as each book of this series offers. In particular, the goal of Volume II in all three of its unique editions, is to offer effective research methods and designs in unique application for doctoral research intended for emerging and beginning doctoral scholars as they structure new research to address emerging questions that society needs answers to move forward. This third edition adds to the other two volumes with additional applications of quantitative, qualitative, and mixed method studies that incorporate a multitude of designs from correlational, to case study, comparative study, additional discussion on use of the Delphi technique, phenomenology, transcendental, the van Kaam method and new emerging model—The Praxis Documentation and Aesthetic Interpretation (PDAI) Model.

How Does Refractive Thinking Benefit Students and Employees?

Individuals within either academia or the business landscape seem to find comfort with what they currently regard as truth. To reiterate, refractive thinking is *beyond perceived* limits of the proverbial box challenging what is current known.

The design of this doctoral series looks toward existing issues and opportunities while suspending judgment, freeing one's mind to be limitless. Refractive thinking goes beyond the rules, simply existing where one suspends and resists any type of confinement, labels, or parameters of any kind. This free-thinking without any convention is something that few truly can obtain.

Einstein was one of the rare few who thought beyond that had not been previously considered. He strove to decipher behavior in a way that did not follow conventional wisdom. Initially, only a select group could grasp the radically different concepts Einstein put forth. Much like during the time of Sir Isaac Newton or perhaps even further when the earth was believed to be flat, these critical thinkers are the pioneers who represent the ideals of refractive thinking.

Descartes offers the often quoted phrase: "*I think therefore I am.*" Allow me to expand this view by adding "I critically think *to be*, I refractively think *to change the world*" (Lentz, 2009, p. xiii). My goal is to help adult learners as emerging researchers and scholars develop their critical thinking skills to see what is already there through a slightly different lens. This new perspective enables them to learn to question everything they see and to have their curiosity drive them to question--*why?*

Refractive thinking embraces the post modernism guise of the ability to hold divergent points of view and theory *simultaneously*. It builds a foundation of duality. Society is uncomfortable with simultaneous duality—the thought that two divergent boundaries can exist and both can be correct—*from their point of view* is challenging to wrap one's arms around. Dealing within not only duality but also multiplicity of meaning is where refractive thinking exists, expands, and offers a new contemplation of thought. The goal is to exist within a modality of asking *why* and *why not*, and to suggest *what if?* The goal is to build the capacity to understanding limitlessness.

What is it that prevents most people from achieving this state? Why is it easier to cling to the safety of the confines of the proverbial box allowing only the dichotomy of opposites, or either or extremes? Instead, why not break this cycle of fear and simply stop? Perhaps the solution is not a box *at all*. Instead, this refractive thinking is a free form that is fluid and dynamic. Can we exist without having to clearly define the parameters of that existence? This is the quest of The Refractive Thinker,[®] to discover the yet unknown and to realize that one cannot put new ideas into old constructs (Senge, 1990).

What Lies Ahead for The Refractive Thinker Series?

Since The Refractive Thinker[®] began in 2009, the Publishing Industry has recognized its efforts winning nine awards thus far; earning prestigious awards from The Next Generation Indie Book Awards, Axiom Business Book Awards, USA Book News Awards, Excellence in Digital Publishing with the eLit Awards, The International Book Awards, as well as earning a QED distinction. As the popularity of the series continues to grow, our goal is to continue to reach out to the doctoral student and faculty, as well as the doctoral scholar to provide a quality peer-reviewed anthology that promotes unique and emerging research to include unique *applications* of research and design. With constant business and social changes, a need exists for people to become *refractive thinkers* who not only *think out-of-the-box*, but who eliminate the need for the concept of a *box*.

INDEX

The Refractive Thinker®

AND

Pensiero Press

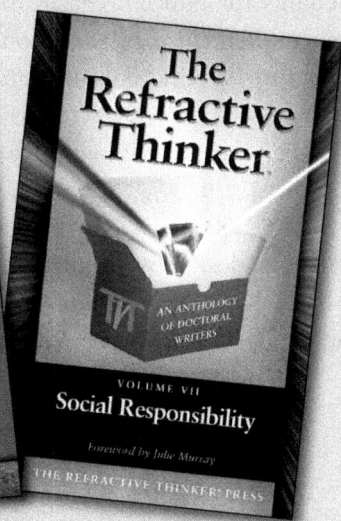

The Refractive Thinker®:
An Anthology of Higher Learning

The Refractive Thinker® Press
9065 Big Plantation Avenue
Las Vegas, NV 89143-5440 USA

info@refractivethinker.com
www.refractivethinker.com
blog: www.dissertationpublishing.com

Books are available through The Refractive Thinker® Press at special discounts for bulk purchases for the purpose of sales promotion, seminar attendance, or educational purposes. Special volumes can be created for specific purposes and to organizational specifications. Orders placed on www.refractivethinker.com for students and military receive a 15% discount. Please contact us for further details.

Refractive Thinker® logo by Joey Root; The Refractive Thinker® Press logo design by Jacqueline Teng, cover design by Peri Poloni-Gabriel, Knockout Design (www.knockoutbooks.com), production by Gary A. Rosenberg (www.thebookcouple.com).

Pensiero Press

Pensiero Press
9065 Big Plantation Avenue
Las Vegas, NV 89143-5440 USA

I *think* therefore I am.

—R<small>ENEE</small> D<small>ESCARTES</small>

I *critically think* to be.
I *refractively think* to change the world.

T<small>HANK YOU FOR JOINING US</small> as we continue to celebrate the accomplishments of doctoral scholars affiliated with many phenomenal institutions of higher learning. The purpose of the anthology series is to share a glimpse into the scholarly works of participating authors on various subjects.

The Refractive Thinker® serves the tenets of leadership, which is not simply a concept outside of the self, but comes from within, defining our very essence; where the search to define leadership becomes our personal journey, not yet a finite destination.

The Refractive Thinker® is an intimate expression of who we are: the ability to think beyond the traditional boundaries of thinking and critical thinking. Instead of mere reflection and evaluation, one challenges the very boundaries of the constructs itself. If thinking is *inside* the box, and critical thinking is *outside* the box, we add the next step of refractive thinking, *beyond* the box. Perhaps the need exists to dissolve the box completely. As in our first four volumes, the authors within these pages are on a mission to change the world. They are never satisfied or quite content with *what is* or asking *why,* instead these authors intentionally strive to push and test the limits to ask *why not.*

We look forward to your interest in discussing future opportunities. Let our collection of authors continue the journey initiated with Volume I, to which *The Refractive Thinker*® will serve as our guide to future volumes. Come join us in our quest to be refractive thinkers and add your wisdom to the collective. We look forward to your stories.

Please contact The Refractive Thinker® Press for information regarding these authors and the works contained within these pages. Perhaps you or your organization may be looking for an author's expertise to incorporate as part of your annual corporate meetings as a keynote or guest speaker(s), perhaps to offer individual, or group seminars or coaching, or require their expertise as consultants.

Join us on our continuing adventures of *The Refractive Thinker®* where we expand the discussion specifically begun in Volume I with leadership; Volume II with Research Methodology (now in its 2nd Edition); Volume III with Change Management; Volume IV with Ethics, Leadership, and Globalization; Volume V with Strategy in Innovation, Volume VI with Post-Secondary Education, and Volume VII with Social Responsibility—all themed to explore the realm of strategic thought, creativity, and innovation.

Dr. Cheryl A. Lentz, managing editor of The Lentz Leadership Institute, explains the unique benefits of the books for readers:

"They celebrate the diffusion of innovative refractive thinking through the writings of these doctoral scholars as they dare to think differently in search of new applications and understandings of research methodology. Unlike most academic books that merely define research, The Refractive Thinker® offers unique applications of research methodologies from the perspective of multiple authors—each offering a chapter based on their specific expertise."

Books from
THE REFRACTIVE THINKER® PRESS

The Refractive Thinker®: Volume I: An Anthology of Higher Learning

The Refractive Thinker®: Volume II: Research Methodology

The Refractive Thinker®: Volume II: Research Methodology, 2nd Edition

The Refractive Thinker®: Volume III: Change Management

The Refractive Thinker®: Volume IV: Ethics, Leadership, and Globalization

The Refractive Thinker®: Volume V: Strategy in Innovation

The Refractive Thinker®: Volume VI: Post-Secondary Education

The Refractive Thinker®: Volume VII: Social Responsibility

Refractive Thinker volumes are available in e-book, Kindle®, iPad®, Nook®, and Sony Reader™, as well as individual e-chapters by author.

COMING SOON!
The Refractive Thinker®: Vol II: Research Methodology 3rd Edition

Telephone orders: Call us at 702 421-6294

Email Orders: orders@lentzleadership.com

Website orders: Please place orders through our website:
www.refractivethinker.com

Postal Orders: The Refractive Thinker® Press
9065 Big Plantation Avenue
Las Vegas, NV 89143-5440 USA

Refractive
Thinker®
Press

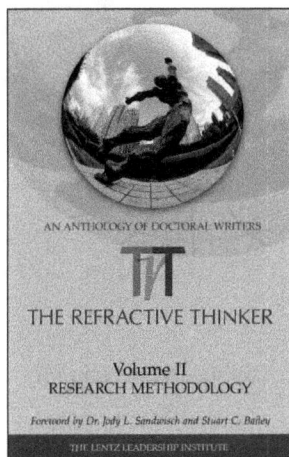

The Refractive Thinker®: Volume II: Research Methodology

The authors within these pages are on a mission to change the world, never satisfied or quite content with what is or asking *why*, instead these authors intentionally strive to push and test the limits to ask *why not*. *The Refractive Thinker®* is an intimate expression of who we are—the ability to think beyond the traditional boundaries of thinking and critical thinking. Instead of mere reflection and evaluation, one challenges the very boundaries of the constructs itself.

The Refractive Thinker®: Volume II: Research Methodology, 2nd Edition

Chosen as Finalist, Education/Academic category The USA "Best Books 2011" Awards, sponsored by USA Book News

As in Volume I, the authors within these pages are on a mission to change the world, never satisfied or quite content with what is or asking *why*, instead these authors intentionally strive to push and test the limits to ask *why not*. *The Refractive Thinker®* is an intimate expression of who we are—the ability to think beyond the traditional boundaries of thinking and critical thinking. Instead of mere reflection and evaluation, one challenges the very boundaries of the constructs itself.

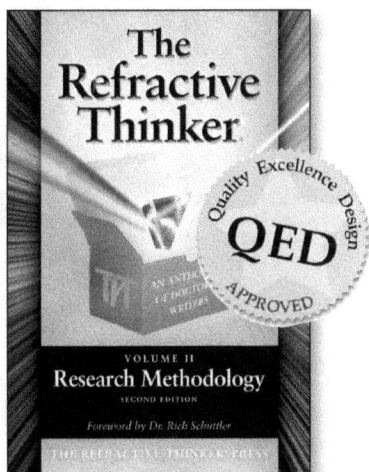

For more information, please visit our website: www.refractivethinker.com

The Refractive Thinker®: Volume III: Change Management

This next offering in the series shares yet another glimpse into the scholarly works of these authors, specifically on the topic of change management. In addition to exploring various aspects of change management, the purpose of *The Refractive Thinker*® is also to serve the tenets of leadership. Leadership is not simply a concept outside of the self, but comes from within, defining our very essence; where the search to define leadership becomes our personal journey, not yet a finite destination.

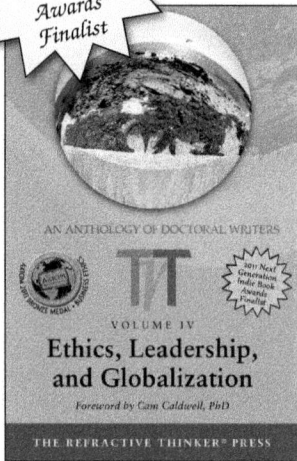

The Refractive Thinker®: Volume IV: Ethics, Leadership, and Globalization

The purpose of this volume is to highlight the scholarly works of these authors on the topics of ethics, leadership, and concerns within the global landscape of business. Join us as we venture forward to showcase the authors of Volume IV, and continue to celebrate the accomplishments of these doctoral scholars affiliated with many phenomenal institutions of higher learning.

For more information, please visit our website: www.refractivethinker.com

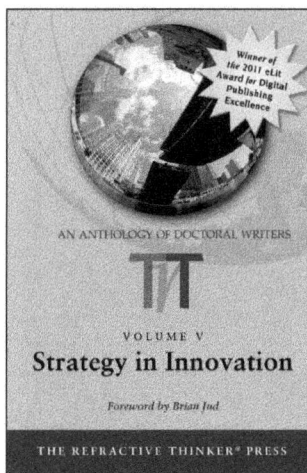

The Refractive Thinker Press Wins 2011 eLit Award for Digital Publishing Excellence

July 2, 2012, Las Vegas, NV—*The Refractive Thinker: Vol. V: Strategy in Innovation* has been named the winner of the Gold in the Anthology category of the 2011 eLit Awards!

The Refractive Thinker®: Volume VI: Post-Secondary Education

Celebrate the diffusion of innovative refractive thinking through the writings of these doctoral scholars as they dare to think differently in search of new applications and understandings of post-secondary education. Unlike most academic books that merely define research, *The Refractive Thinker®* offers commentary regarding the state of post-secondary education from the perspective of multiple authors—each offering a chapter based on their specific expertise.

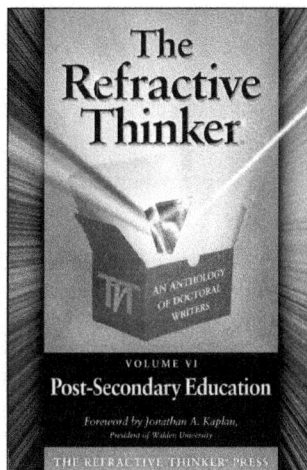

For more information, please visit our website: www.refractivethinker.com

JOURNEY OUTSIDE THE GOLDEN PALACE

DR. CHERYL LENTZ

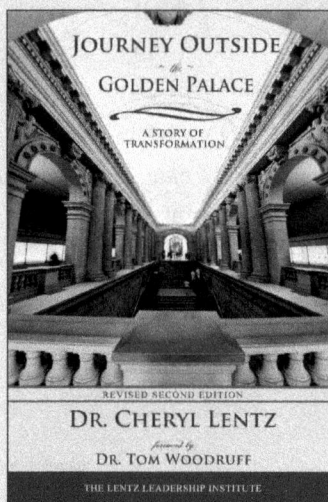

Come take a mythical journey with Henry from *The Village of Yore* and the many colorful characters of The Golden Palace on their quest to unlock the palatial gates of corporate Ivory Towers. This allegorical tale demonstrates the lessons learned when leaders in organizations fail to serve the needs of their stakeholders. Come join us in a journey toward understanding the elegant simplicity of effective leadership, unlocking the secrets to The Golden Palace Theory of Management along the way.

This revised second edition offers a companion workbook for discussion, reflection, and refractive thinking. The purpose of this workbook is to more closely examine each character and their leadership qualities. Take a leap of faith and follow us on our journey. Perhaps you may recognize some old friends on your travels.

Pensiero Press PUBLISHES LANDMARK BOOK ON THE CHANGING ADULT EDUCATION ARENA

2011 Next Generation Indie Book Awards Finalist

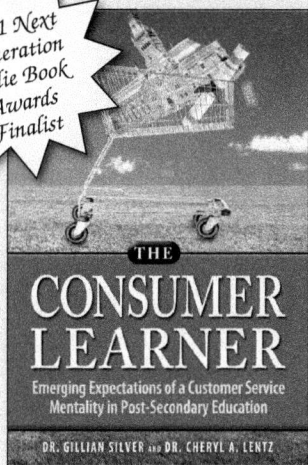

PENSIERO PRESS WINS FINALIST AWARD

May 12, 2012, Las Vegas, NV—*The Consumer Learner* **has been named a Finalist in the Education/Academic category of the 2012 Next Generational Indie Book Awards!**

Anyone who has entered a college classroom in the last 5 years has recognized a clear transformation in the context of higher education. A dynamic revolution in practice and delivery is underway, and the implications of change are ripe for analysis.

Administrators are increasingly charged with revenue production and institutional leadership. Faculty are experimenting with new andragogical models and advances in interactive technology. Students are embracing new modalities as they strive to make curriculum immediately transferable into industry. *The Consumer Learner: Emergence and Expectations of a Customer Service Mentality in Post-Secondary Education* examines the new reality and emerging patterns shaping the experiences of these three diverse, yet interconnected, constituencies.

This book provides a distinctive approach to the transformation of the higher education culture within the U.S. Authors Dr. Gillian Silver and Dr. Cheryl Lentz, noted content experts, professors and curriculum/program developers, explain that the contents will initiate an intensive dialogue about the implications and impacts on administrative structure, faculty practice, and learner outcomes. According to Dr. Lentz, "This is a frank, encompassing work that has the capacity to ignite a national dialogue. We think the review will give voice to the significance of this evolving environment. The voices of experience leading this change will emerge."

Follow the authors on the Web: ww.consumerlearner.com and Blog: www.consumerlearner.com/wordpress/

Available through Pensiero Press, a division of the The Lentz Leadership Institute. $24.95 (HARDCOVER)

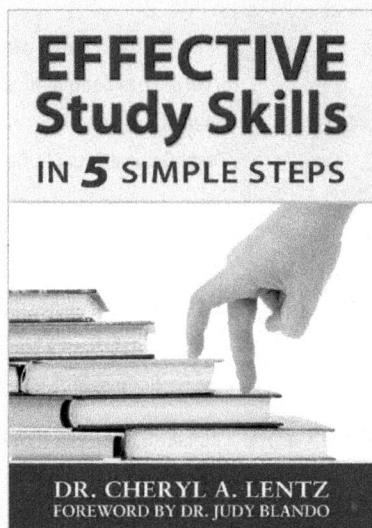

EFFECTIVE
Study Skills
IN **5** SIMPLE STEPS

Dr. Cheryl Lentz has compiled the valuable information she gives in her blog in one easy-to-use handbook. The study tips are designed to help any student improve learning and understanding, and ultimately earn higher grades. The handbook is not so large that it requires long hours of reading, as is the case with many books on the subject. The information is written in a manner to help a learner "see" and "practice" proven study techniques. Effective study skills must be practiced to for improvement to occur.

PUBLICATIONS ORDER FORM

Please send the following books:

❏ *The Refractive Thinker®: Volume I: An Anthology of Higher Learning*
❏ *The Refractive Thinker®: Volume II: Research Methodology*
❏ *The Refractive Thinker®: Volume II: Research Methodology, 2nd Edition*
❏ *The Refractive Thinker®: Volume III: Change Management*
❏ *The Refractive Thinker®: Volume IV: Ethics, Leadership, and Globalization*
❏ *The Refractive Thinker®: Volume V: Strategy in Innovation*
❏ *The Refractive Thinker®: Volume VI: Post-Secondary Education*
❏ *The Refractive Thinker®: Volume VII: Social Responsibility*

Please contact the Refractive Thinker® Press for book prices, e-book prices, and shipping.
Individual e-chapters available by author: $3.95 (plus applicable tax). www.refractivethinker.com

❏ *The Consumer Learner: Emergence and Expectations of a Customer Service Mentality in Post-Secondary Education*

❏ *Effective Study Skills in 5 Simple Steps*

❏ *Journey Outside the Golden Palace*

Please send more FREE information:

❏ Speaking engagements   ❏ Educational seminars   ❏ Consulting

Join our Mailing List

Name: _____

Address:_____

City:_____ State:_____ Zip: _____

Telephone: _____ Email:_____

Sales tax: NV Residents please add 8.1% sales tax

Shipping: *Please see our website for shipping rates.*

Please mail or e-mail form to:

The Refractive Thinker® Press/
  Pensiero Press
9065 Big Plantation Ave.
Las Vegas, NV 89143-5440 USA
E-mail: orders@lentzleadership.com

Yes, I would like to participate in:

❏ **Doctoral Volume**(s) for a specific university or organization:

Name: _____

Contact Person: _____

Telephone: _____ E-mail: _____

❏ **Specialized Volume**(s) Business or Themed:

Name: _____

Contact Person: _____

Telephone: _____ E-mail: _____

Please mail or e-mail form to:

The Refractive Thinker® Press
9065 Big Plantation Ave.
Las Vegas, NV 89143-5440 USA

E-mail: orders@lentzleadership.com
www.refractivethinker.com